D1030128

Appearances and Disappearances

Strange comings and goings from the Bermuda Triangle to the Mary Celeste

Editor: Peter Brookesmith

CHARTWELL
BOOKS, INC.

Acknowledgements
Photographs were supplied by Aldus Archive, Atlantic
Mutual Insurance Company, BBC Hulton Picture Library,
Chris Barker, Paul Begg, Bermuda Tourist Board, Fred
Bost, Boston University Library, British Aerospace, British
Museum, Richard Burgess, Robert Capa/John Hillelson,
Jean-Loup Charmet, Bruce Coleman Ltd, Anne Court,
Daily Telegraph Colour Library, Robert Estall, Mary Evans
Picture Library, Fate Magazine, Werner Forman Archive,
Fortean Picture Library, John Frost Historical Newspaper
Services, Roy Fulton, Leif Griges, Dennis Gifford, John
Glanville, Colin Godman, Granada Publishing, Stuart
Howe, Robert Hunt Library, Imperial War Museum,
Keystone, Kobal Collection, Larry Kusche, Lisbon
Academy of Science, WG Lucas, McDonnell Douglas,
Mansell Collection, Marshall Cavendish, Meteorological
Office/JH Golden, NASA National Archives, National
Gallery of Ireland, National Monuments Record, Peter
Newark's Western Americana, New English Library, North
Carolina Museum of History, Pan Books, Peabody Museum,
Photri, Popperfoto, Press Association, Rex Features,
Rochester Museum, Roger Viollet, SITU, Souvenir Press,
Spectrum Colour Library, John Massey Stewart, Sunn
Classic Productions, John Topham Library, David
Towersey, UPI, Ullstein, US National Archives, J. Worsley,
George Wright.

Consultants:
Professor A J Ellinson
Dr J Allen Hynek
Brian Inglis
Colin Wilson

Contents

Introduction

Introducing the mystery of the disappearance of the British diplomat, Benjamin Bathurst, Charles Fort (pioneer collector of accounts of strange phenomena) wrote: 'Here is the shortest story I know . . . He walked around the horses.' That was all that could be said about the moment, on 25 November 1809, when Bathurst examined the coach horses prior to resuming his journey home to England from the court of Emperor Francis at Vienna. Outside an inn in the small German town of Perleberg, and in full view of his valet and secretary, Bathurst stepped around the horses and off the face of this earth.

Ultimately, not much more can be said about the truly mysterious disappearance, or its counterpart, the inexplicable and sudden appearance, of a person or object from or into the world. Indeed, as a useful index I have often found that the probable verity of a case is in inverse proportion to the authentic details available about its crucial moment. After all, a sudden disappearance takes its essential evidence with it, and in noticing the vacuum even the keenest of observers would sooner or later begin to doubt their own eyes.

Those who witness or stumble upon an appearance are more fortunate in being able to grasp or interrogate their material evidence, although most usually, as in the celebrated case of Kaspar Hauser, the cryptic information they receive only adds to their confusion. Those who appear are usually less fortunate still, as illustrated by the following fatal example, told to the English philosopher, John Aubrey, by an acquaintance who heard of the case while in Portugal in 1655. As Aubrey records it in his *Miscellanies*, a Portuguese man was tried by the Inquisition following his unexplained appearance in that country. I say 'unexplained' because the man himself could not say why or how he came to be there. He had been about his business, in the Portuguese colony of Goa, in India, when suddenly, as far as he could tell, he was back in Portugal. What little he could say was that he must have been 'brought thither . . . in the air, in an incredible short time.' This sounds like levitation, spontaneous flight or even teleportation to our wonder-thirsty age; but in the dark age of its happening, fear was spreading over Europe as the light of reason was blotted out by the smoke from witch-burnings. The man who had survived his magical translation from India to Portugal was found guilty of consorting with the Devil, tied to a fiery stake, and given a public send-off on a longer journey from which he could never return.

In his wide-ranging study of a bewildering variety of reports of paranormal and unexplained phenomena, Fort encountered many forms of appearances and disappearances. In particular he noted the comings and goings of objects that the spiritualists call apports, but his fact gathering showed many instances in which the attributing of these mysterious journeys to the actions of discarnate entities was not only inappropriate, its 'special pleading' was also an obstacle to any more accurate understanding of what was going on. For his *Book of the Damned*, in 1919, Fort coined the less emotive term 'teleportation' to describe – not explain – the hypothetical force by which objects and people could be transported, presumably instantaneously, from one place to another, and again presumably without necessarily traversing the intervening physical distance. If teleportation existed, argued Fort, it would show up, mostly indirectly, in data about objects or people mysteriously disappearing or appearing. This exists in abundance, if looked for in the right places.

Take conventional 'missing persons' statistics, for example. We are told that in London alone, the Metropolitan Police receives on average more than fifty calls a day. In most cases the person turns up, or is traced one way or another, but an alarming seven vanish without trace in London every day. General statistics for the year 1977, cited by Paul Begg in his *Into Thin Air*, suggest that UK disappearances may reach a quarter of a million. It would not be unreasonable to believe that this figure has been exceeded, here in the mid-1980s, and that the world-wide total would be several orders larger if it were at all calculable. There are many reasons for wanting to vanish – family and marriage problems figure most highly. It seems that a few turn up in mental institutions, a greater number fall prey to drugs, crime and murder, and a large percentage, it must be assumed, have no wish to be found.

From our modern standpoint we must take into account the mental phenomenon of fugue states (loss of sense of identity) and secondary personalities, the classic example of which, recorded by the pioneering American psychologist, William James, involved the Rev. Ansel Bourne, of Rhode Island, U.S.A. On January 17, 1887, Bourne withdrew some money from a bank in Providence, paid some bills, got into a horse-drawn tram and vanished. About two months later, a man calling himself A.J. Brown, who had recently rented a small shop in Norristown, Pennsylvania, woke up in confusion, his frightened calls bringing the other people in the shared building. He did not know where he was and insisted his name was Ansel Bourne. On his return to his Rhode Island family, Bourne was weak, having lost twenty pounds in weight, and had no recollection of what he had done between stepping into the tram and waking up in Norristown. Three years later James met Bourne and under hypnosis brought forward the 'A.J. Brown' personality, complete with its memory of the missing weeks.

Recent studies have shown that similar amnesic states may be more common than is generally believed; for not only can fugue states last from several seconds to a number of years, but whereas Bourne regained his identity spontaneously, some do not, remaining lost to their wives, children and friends, even if they are accidentally discovered in their new lives. Besides the psychological pressures or conflicts which produce such dramatic hysterical dissociations of personality, similar effects can be caused by head injuries, or by other kinds of brain damage which may result variously from disease or strokes, poisoning by over-indulgence in drugs or drink, extreme fatigue, epilepsy or even schizophrenia. Any one of these might produce alternating personalities, fugue and amnesia, and become the background to an intriguing story of a disappearance or appearance. Although the mechanism of this psychological phenomenon still eludes today's witch-doctors, how much more mysterious it must have seemed to people in earlier times.

When facing the difficulty of explaining strange phenomena, it is not hard to imagine how satisfying it was to look for answers in the twilight world of witches and demons, spirits and fairies, and in the whole folklore of changelings and spirit possession. And lest we think we are superior to our medieval forebears, these themes are just as alive today in the UFO myths of abduction by aliens. Indeed, it seems that if stories of bizarre disappearances did not exist, the fertile human imagination would create – or in psycho-mythological terms, *re-create* – them. This is shown in this volume with the example of how successive variations have been published of the entirely fictitious story of a boy who vanished (his footprints in the snow stopping suddenly) on the way to a farmyard well. This was said to have taken place on Christmas Eve 1876, or 1889, or 1890, depending on which version you read.

There is an issue lurking here which has been the bane of every serious researcher into the genre of appearances and disappearances. It is that many of the writers of popular books on UFOs and Fortean mysteries in the 1960s and 70s were careless in their verification of stories, grabbing material indiscriminately from the most dubious of sources. Some even deliberately fabricated or distorted data to fit their notions. The consequence was that a great many preposterous stories went into general circulation, and it has taken many tedious hours of research to separate the fiction from any kernel of fact. The classic example of this is the legend of the vanishing regiment in the campaign at Gallipoli in 1915, and of the strange cloud that was said to have swept it away. The story was used shamelessly in later UFO books to show how cunningly alien machines can disguise themselves as they carry out their nefarious abductions of unwary earthlings. You will read the true story in this volume, but the irony is that the UFO version will undoubtedly live on.

Harder and even more time-consuming to unravel are the open-ended enigmas such as the notorious Bermuda Triangle, and the so-called 'Philadelphia Experiment' (which allegedly demonstrated the phenomena of invisibility and teleportation) because they are vast and ill-defined. In both cases the sparse facts are obscured by a heavy smokescreen of lies, rumours, omissions and distortions which has been created by unscrupulous writers to back up a web of occult and speculative science fiction posing as fact. In the case of the Bermuda Triangle there have indeed been some unexplained disappearances, but no more or less, it seems, than could be expected in any other busy shipping area, and in numbers which reflect only the large amount of traffic within an area of generally unpredictable and extreme weather and ocean conditions.

Much in the same vein is the disappearance in 1587 of the population of Roanoke, a small English colony on the coast of North Carolina, about which there has been much fantastic speculation. Paul Begg, the intrepid researcher who has battled to the heart of many of the classic mysteries described in this volume, writes herein: 'The Roanoke disappearance *is*

a mystery, but only insofar as there is no absolute proof of the colonists' fate and not because of any suggestion that their disappearance was in even the slightest way paranormal or supernatural.' The same could probably be said of one of the world's favourite and more genuine mysteries: the fate of the crew of the *Mary Celeste* (not *Marie Celeste* as many books wrongly have it). We simply don't know what happened to them, and that makes it more of an authentic vanishing mystery than tales of kidnap by a marauding UFO, attack by a sea serpent, or a slip into another dimension, all of which explanations of the mystery are no more than guesswork.

It would be easy to judge all the stories in this volume, either accept or dismiss them, and place them on a spectrum ranging between fact and fiction. But to do this would be ignoring the fact that they are more than one-dimensional. Right or wrong, true or false, the incidents of appearance and disappearance described here have become part of contemporary folklore. An excellent example is the continuing phenomenon of 'phantom hitch-hikers'. Once studied only in the light of local folklore, we now know that reports of this phenomenon can be found all over the world and in every century. Folklorists have studied the genre in the hope of revealing the origin of the idea and how it travelled, but it is so universal they now accept that it has sprung up independently at different times and places. Given their evidence, some believe it therefore to be an example of a mythological archetype, whose true origin lies in the human unconscious and whose true meaning is found in the realm of psychological symbology. And here is another mystery; we also have seemingly real events to go on, with eye-witness testimony, suggesting that this particular branch of folklore is continuously and spontaneously recreated in daily life.

While Charles Fort rather jokingly proposed that, if teleportation existed, there could be many people on this earth who have come from other worlds, a more disturbing idea has originated in the ancient religious and philosophical system of Tibet, which many contemporary researchers into the paranormal are taking more seriously. It is the idea of the *tulpa*, a phantom form of a human being, indistinguishable in all respects from the real thing, but created by the power of thought and imagination alone. If tulpas do exist, some of the people in this world of ours may not be real in the same way that we think of ourselves as real; they may come and go in 'unnatural' ways which give rise to the kind of stories represented here.

In the legends of many peoples, their heroes have passed into other worlds, some permanently, ascending to celestial regions or descending into the underworld. These themes are dramatized symbolically in the shaman's trance and are thus universally familiar. As we have seen, in our materialistic age a man can simply vanish. But in the archaic world in which the shaman had a fundamental social, spiritual and psychological function, the event had a significance for all men. A man may have disappeared from mortal ken, but that only meant his spirit was beyond us in a greater life, peopled with gods and demons, wizards and elementals. It should not surprise us then, that when Colonel Percy Fawcett failed to come back from exploring the Amazon in 1925; when Flight 19 took off into oblivion on its disastrous training mission over Florida in 1945; when 'Princess Caraboo' appeared in Bristol in 1817; and Kaspar Hauser was found at the gates of Nuremburg in 1828, *ad infinitum,* whatever the facts were, the mundane event was blasted into mythological perpetuity by the human imagination.

BOB RICKARD

The mysterious disappearance of ships and aircraft in an area of the North Atlantic has led to the belief that the region is host to strange and powerful hostile forces. PAUL BEGG gives the background to the legend

MERE MENTION of the Bermuda Triangle is likely to enliven any flagging conversation and set people's spines tingling almost anywhere in the world. It has been the subject of books, novels, films, television dramas and documentaries, newspaper and magazine articles – even a board game. The Bermuda Triangle – formed by an imaginary line connecting Bermuda with Puerto Rico and the coast of Florida – is the place where scores of ships and aircraft are said to have vanished without trace. Dozens of researchers and writers are convinced that the losses are caused by some kind of force or phenomenon unknown to science.

Charles Berlitz, author of two best-sellers about the region, *The Bermuda Triangle* and *Without a trace*, has written:

Large and small boats have disappeared without leaving wreckage, as if they and their crews had been snatched into another dimension . . . in no other area have the unexplained disappearances been so numerous, so well recorded, so sudden, and attended by such unusual circumstances, some of

Above: Charles Berlitz has done most to foster the idea that disappearances in the Bermuda Triangle are the result of extraordinary happenings

Below: the island of Bermuda in the Atlantic. Is it at the centre of a whole series of sinister events?

which push the element of coincidence to the borders of impossibility.
'The number of disappearances are out of all proportion to the number of losses elsewhere,' writes Ivan T. Sanderson in *Invisible residents*. And John Wallace Spencer claims in *Limbo of the lost*: 'Tragedies connected with this region continually occur without explanation, without pattern, without warning, and without reason.'

Bermuda has had an evil reputation for generations. Its 300 or so tiny islands were discovered in 1515 by Juan de Bermúdez. Yet, despite an equitable climate, plentiful supplies of fresh food and water, and an ideal location for a mid-ocean refuge and provisioning base, the islands were shunned for almost a century after their discovery. They were feared by the tough Elizabethan sailors, Shakespeare called them 'the still-vex'd Bermoothes', and they gained an evil reputation as a place of devils. Nobody knows why. Perhaps the only reasonable explanation is that then, as now, the region was known as the home of inexplicable forces that made men and ships disappear.

According to writers on the subject, the modern catalogue of losses in the region begins in 1800 with the disappearance of the USS *Pickering*. In 1854 the British ship *Bella* disappeared en route from Rio de Janeiro to Jamaica, although she was known to have

Tales from the Bermuda Triangle

been dangerously overloaded and may simply have capsized. In 1866 the Triangle claimed the Swedish barque *Lotta* and two years later the Spanish merchantman *Viego* vanished. In 1872 the crew of the *Mary Celeste* disappeared and the vessel was found drifting between the Azores and Gibraltar (see page 76). Although this is far outside the accepted limits of the Bermuda Triangle, the *Mary Celeste* is often referred to in discussion of the subject. The British training ship *Atalanta* and her 290 cadets and crew sailed into oblivion in 1880. They were followed in 1884 by the Italian schooner *Miramon*.

It is said that in 1902 the German barque *Freya*, sailing from Manzanillo in Cuba to Punta Arenas, Chile, was found in the Triangle. Her crew had disappeared. The vessel itself was listing badly, was partly dismasted and showed every sign of having been caught in a particularly violent storm – but there had not been any storms; weather records revealed that only light airs had prevailed.

In 1918 the large collier *Cyclops* mysteriously vanished. She had carried a radio but no distress message had been received. A message *was* sent by the Japanese freighter *Raifuku Maru* in 1925 but it only intensified the mystery because the radio operator is reported as saying: 'Danger like dagger now. Come quick!' What kind of danger looks like a dagger? Was dagger the only comparison the terrified radio operator could draw to the unworldly something that threatened and eventually took his ship? Thirteen years later, in 1938, the blue skies were cloudless and the sea was still when the steamship *Anglo-Australian* radioed an 'all's well'

Above: Ivan T. Sanderson has suggested that the Bermuda Triangle is one of 12 'vile vortices' on Earth, regions where the rate of disappearance of ships and aircraft is unusually high

Below: the Bermuda Triangle is usually represented as a region touching Florida and the islands of Puerto Rico and Bermuda. But some writers extend it much further and refer to it as the 'Devil's Triangle' and 'Limbo of the Lost'

message before sailing into the Bermuda Triangle. She never emerged.

Although the Bermuda Triangle has been claiming ships since the days when Christopher Columbus sailed its waters, it did not begin to attract attention until 1945. That year five US Navy bombers – Flight 19 – vanished after sending a series of baffling and bizarre radio messages. A few years later the writer Vincent Gaddis called the region the Bermuda Triangle. There is little agreement among writers on its size and shape, and each region is given a different name such as Devil's Triangle and Limbo of the Lost. At its smallest, however, the Bermuda Triangle is the size of the United Kingdom and Eire, and at its largest it takes in about half the North Atlantic Ocean.

Charles Berlitz and other writers such as Richard Winer, John Wallace Spencer, Vincent Gaddis, John Godwin, Ivan T. Sanderson, Adi-Kent Thomas Jeffrey and Alan Landsberg maintain that the mystery of the Triangle cannot be explained by storms and other natural causes. They believe that the disappearances were caused by a phenomenon unknown to orthodox science.

Vanishing aircraft

In January 1948 the British airliner *Star Tiger* was nearing the end of a routine flight from the Azores to Bermuda when she is said to have radioed: 'Weather and performance excellent. Expect to arrive on schedule.' But the aircraft did not arrive at all. While a search was being made for survivors or wreckage, radio stations picked up a couple of faint messages purporting to be from the aircraft. It was 'as if the final message was being sent or relayed from a far greater

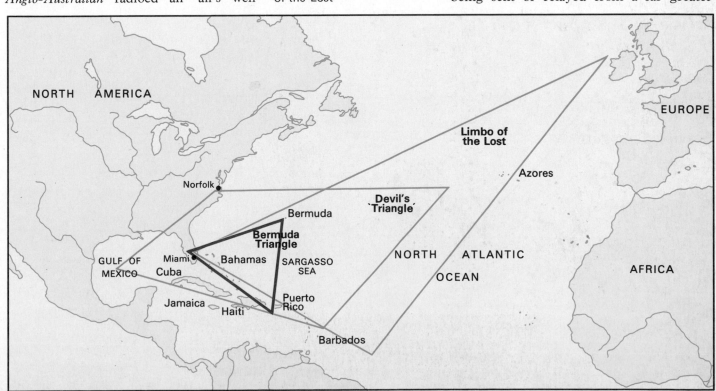

Left: the coast of Florida in 1563, as shown on a map by Lazaro Luis. Christopher Columbus travelled through the area now known as the Bermuda Triangle in the late 15th century and noted that his ship's compass acted erratically. He also recorded that a 'great flame of fire' fell into the sea

Below: an Avenger torpedo bomber of the type that vanished in December 1945 after leaving Fort Lauderdale naval air base for a brief training flight off the Florida coast. No trace of the five aircraft and 14 crew was ever found, despite an extensive search. This case, one of the most celebrated mysteries of aviation history, has been called 'the *Mary Celeste* of the sky'

Bermuda Triangle. It seemed that something prevented the satellite transmitting information to receiving stations. 'We are talking about a force we know nothing about,' Meshejian is quoted as saying.

Even more alarming is the claim that the Bermuda Triangle is not unique. The late Ivan T. Sanderson plotted the location of dozens of air and sea losses and concluded that at least 12 similar regions – he called them 'vile vortices' – encircle our globe. 'Planes, ships, and subs have, as we have stressed, been disappearing all over the world,' he wrote in his book *Invisible residents*, 'but it has to be admitted that many more are reported to have done so in these . . . areas than in any others.'

One such 'vile vortex' has long been known to lie off the coast of Japan. Called the Devil's Sea, it has been claiming small fishing craft of doubtful stability for hundreds of years. Between 1950 and 1954 no less than nine large coastal freighters went missing. The authorities were so alarmed that in 1955 they dispatched a team of scientists aboard the survey ship *Kaiyo Maru No. 5* to investigate the region. To everybody's horror the *Kaiyo Maru No. 5* and her scientists and crew inexplicably vanished. As a consequence the Japanese declared the region an official danger zone.

Unlike their Japanese counterparts the United States authorities have not declared the Bermuda Triangle a danger zone. Indeed, they deny that anything at all unusual is happening there. This official view, however, does not accord with private opinions expressed in unguarded moments. One Navy spokesman let slip: 'We know there's something strange going on out there,

distance, in space or time,' wrote Charles Berlitz.

Another airliner, a Douglas DC-3, vanished on a flight from Puerto Rico to Florida in December 1948. The pilot allegedly radioed: 'We are approaching the field . . . only fifty miles [80 kilometres] to the south. . . . We can see the lights of Miami now . . . all's well. Will stand by for landing instructions.' But when Miami replied a few minutes later she received no reply. Not another word was ever heard from the aircraft. The DC-3 had vanished over an area where the water was only 20 feet (6 metres) deep, yet search craft failed to locate any wreckage or survivors.

In June 1950 in calm seas and in good weather the Costa Rican freighter *Sandra* and her crew of 28 vanished. 'What could have happened to her? No one has the least idea,' says Adi-Kent Thomas Jeffrey.

The extent of the Triangle's range of influence startled researchers when Professor Wayne Meshejian announced that a sophisticated weather satellite operated by the National Oceanographic Administration consistently malfunctioned when over the

we've always known it, but there doesn't seem to be any reason for it at all.' And a senior intelligence officer of the Third Naval District is on record as saying: 'Nobody in the Navy sneers at this thing.' The authorities, it seems, are engaged in a cover-up to conceal their ignorance from the public.

There is little agreement about what 'this thing' in the Bermuda Triangle is. John Wallace Spencer is convinced that UFOS provide the only acceptable solution. Ships and aircraft 'are actually being taken away from our planet,' he says. Looking down instead of up, Ivan T. Sanderson suggested that a highly intelligent civilisation may have evolved on or below the sea bed and that the disappearances are connected with their periodic examination of mankind.

Other suggestions have ranged from mini black holes to openings to other dimensions where time runs quickly, slowly or not at all. That this latter theory may not be as absurd as it sounds is indicated by the experience of a young pilot named Bruce Gernon. In 1970 he was piloting his small aircraft when he flew through a strange cloud. On landing at Miami he discovered that his flight had taken half an hour less than it was possible for it to have done. Did Gernon fly into another dimension and out again? Unfortunately, his flight plan is missing and there is no way of

Above: the United States nuclear submarine *Scorpion* sank in May 1968 with the loss of her 99 crew southwest of the Azores. Although this is far outside the usual limits of the Bermuda Triangle the *Scorpion* is regularly included among its victims. A court of enquiry was unable to explain the sinking

Left: Gibbs Hill lighthouse has acted as a navigational aid on Bermuda since the 1840s. Has it also, in the years since then, been a silent witness of strange disappearances in the surrounding seas?

checking and corroborating his story.

A similar happening is said to have been experienced by the passengers and crew of an Eastern Airlines aircraft that vanished from the radar at Miami for 10 minutes. Full emergency operations were launched but then the airliner reappeared and landed safely. Nobody on board had experienced anything odd and they had no explanation for the fact that every clock and watch on board was found to be 10 minutes slow.

Charles Berlitz believes that the remains of the fabled lost continent of Atlantis have been found off Bimini in the Bahamas. Many people believe that Atlantis was the home of a technological super race and that one of their machines or weapons is still functioning, disintegrating our ships and aircraft.

'Could magnetism or some form of magnetic phenomenon be related to the strange disappearances?' asks Richard Winer, author of *The Devil's Triangle*. Few writers have failed to mention how the compass needle usually points to the magnetic north pole rather than to the actual North Pole – except, however, in the Bermuda Triangle.

The Bermuda Triangle is clearly a strange place and strange things happen there. Hundreds of ships and aircraft have inexplicably vanished without trace. They hardly ever send a distress call and wreckage is rarely found. Furthermore, as John Godwin has written in *This baffling world*, 'we find that almost monotonously fine weather conditions prevailed at the crucial times.' He goes on to ask: 'Did the lost airplanes and lost ships encounter phenomena unknown to today's science? Do the laws of nature still contain a few paragraphs not covered in our textbooks?' We shall see.

Numerous tales of people, boats and aircraft vanishing without trace have been gathered by writers about the Bermuda Triangle to support their view that something weird is happening there. But how strong is their evidence?

THE BERMUDA TRIANGLE, an area of the western Atlantic where scores of ships and aircraft have disappeared without trace, has been described as one of the greatest true-life mysteries of all time. This is not simply because ships and aircraft have vanished there, but because – according to numerous writers and researchers – the disappearances are without explanation and must be caused by some 'force' or phenomenon unknown to science.

It is a very disturbing if not highly alarming claim, and there is little reassurance in the knowledge that the chances of disappearing in the Bermuda Triangle are less than for being killed while crossing the road. Precautions can be taken against the known dangers of the highway, but not against the unknown forces of the Bermuda Triangle. Every crossing of the region is potentially fatal, rather like every pull of the trigger in Russian roulette.

Few writers agree about the precise size and shape of the Bermuda Triangle. Richard Winer thinks it is a trapezium while John Wallace Spencer sees it as a scalene triangle;

Sunk without trace

The *Cyclops*, a US Navy collier, disappeared in March 1918 after leaving Barbados for the Chesapeake Bay area of the eastern USA. The vessel, 540 feet (165 metres) long, carried a crew of about 300 and was laden with manganese ore

Ivan T. Sanderson calls it 'a sort of funny blob'.

The number of disappearances is far from alarmingly high, as some writers contend. About 150,000 boats cross the Bermuda Triangle every year and on average about 10,000 send a distress call. However, only about 100 losses are recorded annually. While 100 losses are 100 too many it is not a significant proportion of 150,000 – 0.07 per cent, in fact.

As well as being subject to all the natural hazards of the sea – such as storms, hurricanes and waterspouts – the Triangle is the home of the Gulf Stream, a fast-moving body of water that can carry an unwary or inexperienced sailor miles off course in a matter of hours and quickly disperse wreckage.

However, when all is said and done, the backbone of the Triangle legend is that catalogue of disappearances and the claim that they defy rational explanation. Charles Berlitz, the best-known of many people who have written about the area, has stated that

All ship losses are mysterious inasmuch as relatively few captains set out to lose their ships. When the fate of a ship is established, or even assumed, the mystery ceases. This has not been the case with the many ships which have disappeared in the Sargasso Sea.

It is there, or near there, that the majority of Bermuda Triangle losses have taken place, he says.

Let us now examine a random sample of

Left: disappearances in the Bermuda Triangle number about 100 annually. This reward poster drew attention to the mysterious fate of the yacht *Saba Bank*, which vanished while sailing from Nassau to Miami in April 1974

Below: the British freighter *Cyclops*, which went missing in the North Atlantic during the Second World War. It could have been torpedoed, but Charles Berlitz maintains that records show no German submarines to have been in the area when the ship disappeared

Bottom: the ss *Marine Sulphur Queen* left Beaumont, Texas, on 2 February 1963 bound for Norfolk, Virginia. She carried a cargo of molten sulphur and was last heard from on 4 February. An official investigation said the ship could have sunk because of an explosion, could have capsized in heavy seas, or its hull may have broken in two

famous case of the Richard Tichborne inheritance. This ship did not disappear without trace. Wreckage from the vessel is said to have been found six days after she had left Rio, so assuming perfect sailing conditions and maximum speed, the nearest she could have been to the Bermuda Triangle when disaster struck was some 2000 miles (3200 kilometres) away.

A similar case is that of the German barque *Freya*. She is said to have sailed from Manzanillo, Cuba, in 1902 and to have been found in the Triangle abandoned by her crew and giving every appearance of having been caught in a particularly violent storm. Weather records apparently reveal that only light airs prevailed in the region at the time. The *Freya* was, however, in an area where submarine volcanic activity had been reported at about the same time as the ship was abandoned, and it is believed that this prompted the crew to abandon ship. Whether or not this explanation is correct does not really matter because the *Freya* did not sail from Manzanillo, Cuba, but from Manzanillo, Mexico, and she was not found abandoned in the Bermuda Triangle, nor even in the Atlantic Ocean, but in the Pacific.

No hint of mystery was ever attached to either the *Bella* or the *Freya* until writers began searching for Triangle fatalities. Other ships – the *Lotta*, *Viego*, and *Miramon* or *Miramonde* – could not be traced by this writer and it is questionable whether they ever existed.

In the 19th and early 20th centuries, ships did not carry radio equipment. We cannot be certain of where they were when disaster struck or of what form the disaster took. For example, the *Atalanta* (not *Atlanta* as many authors call her) disappeared on an intended voyage of 3000 miles (4800 kilometres), only 500 miles (800 kilometres) of which were through the Bermuda Triangle. We do not know where she was when she was overwhelmed, but we do know that she had a crew of very inexperienced cadets and that severe storms swept her route.

The first radio-carrying vessel claimed by

Triangle fatalities. The British ship *Bella* is said to have vanished in 1854 on a voyage from Rio de Janeiro to Jamaica. She is known to have been overloaded and is presumed to have capsized, but author Alan Landsberg has wondered why the vessel should have had a safe voyage until she entered the deadly Triangle.

The writer of this article has been unable to identify the *Bella*. Lloyd's have a record of a ship of that name built in Liverpool in 1852, but there is no suggestion that it suffered any misfortune. The only ship corresponding with the Triangle's *Bella* is a vessel of that name that is sometimes associated with the

Berlitz's own words: 'When the fate of a ship is established, or even assumed, the mystery ceases.'

The cornerstone of the Triangle myth is the disappearance of five US Navy bombers – Flight 19 – and a sea plane, all on 5 December 1945, and this will be the subject of a future chapter. Among other aircraft to have vanished in the Bermuda Triangle were the British airliner *Star Tiger* and a Douglas DC-3, both in 1948.

The *Star Tiger*, a Tudor IV aircraft, mysteriously vanished towards the end of a flight from the Azores to Bermuda on 30 January of that year. Contrary to the Triangle legend, the last message from it was an acknowledgement of a radio bearing requested several minutes earlier and not 'Weather and performance excellent. Expect to arrive on schedule.' The weather, in fact, was anything but excellent. Cloud cover throughout the flight had prevented accurate navigation; and the aircraft had battled severe headwinds, forcing the pilot to revise

the Bermuda Triangle was the 19,000-tonne collier *Cyclops* in March 1918. As with the *Atalanta*, her route was in the path of a severe storm, winds reaching peak speeds of 84 miles per hour (135 km/h). It is quite likely that she capsized. Her top-heavy superstructure and the nature of her cargo – which may not have been properly secured – would have ensured that the *Cyclops* sank very quickly indeed.

The Japanese freighter *Raifuku Maru* is said to have vanished in 1925 after sending a strange radio message: 'Danger like dagger now. Come quick!' The message, picked up by the White Star liner *Homeric* but distorted by electrical interference, was in fact 'Now very danger. Come quick!' The *Homeric* sped to the freighter's assistance but encountered mountainous seas and saw the *Raifuku Maru* sink with all hands.

The Triangle writers say that the 355-foot (106-metre) freighter *Sandra* and her crew of 28 sailed into oblivion in calm seas and under blue skies in June 1950. About the only details they get correct are the freighter's name and nationality. The *Sandra* was 185 feet (55 metres) long, carried a crew of 11 and vanished in hurricane force winds in April 1950.

Hurricanes and storms also prevailed when the freighter *Anglo-Australian* vanished in 1938, when the yacht *Connemara IV* was abandoned in 1955, and when the *Revonoc* and its owner Harvey Conover disappeared in 1958. Similar explanations are available for the bulk of Triangle disappearances. Although it is impossible to say for certain that the *Revonoc*, for example, was engulfed by a storm, storms are known to have been responsible for maritime disasters, and the presence of a storm enables us to assume a rational explanation. At which point it is worth remembering Charles

Hurricanes and storms provide likely reasons for some of the losses in the Bermuda Triangle. The *Connemara IV* (above) was found drifting and abandoned in September 1955 off Bermuda. The crew were probably lost overboard when the yacht was caught in a hurricane. The racing yawl *Revonoc* (right) vanished between Key West and Miami in early 1958 when the Florida coast was being battered by near-hurricane-force winds

Below: A Douglas DC-3 of the type that vanished in December 1948

his estimated time of arrival and reducing the safety margin of extra fuel. The airliner disappeared at the most critical stage of her flight. She had insufficient fuel to reach any airport other than Bermuda and was forced to fly at 2000 feet (600 metres) because of the headwinds. Had anything gone wrong such as fuel exhaustion, complete electrical failure or engine breakdown the *Star Tiger* would have plummeted into the sea within seconds.

Omissions and distortions

The case of the Douglas DC-3 lost on 28 December 1948 is an example of how facts have been omitted and distorted to imply a greater mystery than exists. The aircraft, carrying 27 passengers, had left San Juan, Puerto Rico, bound for Miami, Florida. The pilot, Captain Robert Linquist, is said to have radioed that he was 50 miles (80 kilometres) from Miami, could see the lights of the city, and was standing by for landing instructions. Miami replied within minutes, but the aircraft had vanished. The water over which the aircraft was flying was only 20 feet (6 metres) deep, yet search craft failed to locate any wreckage.

The DC-3 is known to have had a defective radio (though some writers have failed to mention this), so the sudden silence does not mean that the aircraft was overcome immediately after sending the message to Miami. It also removes any mystery attached to the lack of a distress call. Furthermore, the pilot did not say he could see the lights of Miami. It seems that some writers have put these words in the pilot's mouth because he said that he was only 50 miles (80 kilometres) from Miami (from which distance the lights of the city would be visible).

However, the pilot had been compensating for a north-west wind, but the wind direction had changed during the flight and it is not known whether the pilot received notification of the fact. If not, he could have missed the Florida Peninsula and literally flown into the Gulf of Mexico. And although the depth of the sea over which the DC-3 was flying at the time of the last message is in places only 20 feet (6 metres) deep, in other areas it plunges to depths of up to 5000 feet (1520 metres). Nobody is certain where the aircraft went down.

Every air disaster is the subject of an exhaustive enquiry to establish the cause. These investigations rely largely on minute examination of wreckage. If there is no wreckage, it is virtually impossible to hazard a guess at what happened. Since none of the accepted causes of an air crash can positively be eliminated nobody can claim that some unknown phenomenon was alone responsible.

A few years ago it was claimed that the strange forces of the Bermuda Triangle reached into space. It was learned that a weather satellite malfunctioned over the Bermuda Triangle and *only* over the Triangle.

In fact the satellite was not malfunctioning. The satellite collected visual and infra-red data on cloud cover and transmitted the information to Earth. For convenience the infra-red signal was transmitted direct while the visual signal was stored on a loop of tape for later transmission. At certain times the tape became full and had to be rewound, so no visual signal was transmitted. By pure coincidence the tape was rewinding when the satellite's orbit brought it over the Triangle.

Then there was the Eastern Airlines aircraft that is said to have disappeared from the radar for 10 minutes and landed at Miami, when every clock and watch aboard was found to be 10 minutes slow. The flight number and the date and time of this event are never given and there is no record of the incident with the FAA, Miami Airport or Eastern Airlines. In short, there is not a scrap of evidence that it ever happened.

The *Star Tiger*, an aircraft of the Tudor IV type (below), went missing in 1948 on a flight from London to Havana via the Azores and Bermuda. The last message received from her gave no inkling of anything untoward

The disappearance of the *Star Tiger* has been called 'truly a modern mystery of the air'. A thorough search of the seas failed to find any trace of the aircraft or its passengers

TUDOR LOST BETWEEN AZORES AND BERMUDA

AIR-SEA RESCUE SEARCH FOR 31 ON BOARD

FROM OUR OWN CORRESPONDENT
NEW YORK, Friday.

All aircraft and ships in the vicinity of Bermuda to-day joined in the search for the British South American Airways Tudor IV., Star Tiger, which is overdue at Bermuda from the Azores.

The search was fully maintained until darkness fell, when the United States Navy recalled all its planes. American Army Flying Fortresses and Super-Fortresses, however, continued their quest during the night, assisted by two British South American Airways machines.

The Star Tiger left London on Tuesday, but was held up by bad weather in the Azores. It was due at Kindley Field, Bermuda, at 5 a.m. G.M.T. to-day.

According to New York Coastguard H.Q. the Star Tiger was 380 miles north-east of Bermuda when its last radio message was received at 3 a.m. The pilot reported nothing unusual.

The plane, which had a crew of

SEARCH PLANE CRASHES : NINE DEAD IN ALPS

LOST DAKOTA SEEN

FROM OUR OWN CORRESPONDENT
PARIS, Friday.

While searching for the American Dakota which crashed in the

Stories about mysterious vanishings in the Bermuda Triangle and Devil's Sea have been fostered by numerous writers who have suggested fantastic explanations. So what can we believe about this legend?

New angle on the Triangle

WHEN EXAMINED CLOSELY the only mystery about the Bermuda Triangle is how it came to be believed in. Both research and reasoning leave much to be desired, as is illustrated by Ivan T. Sanderson's contention that no less than 12 'vile vortices' encircle the globe. The impression given by Sanderson and other writers is that the existence of these 'vile vortices' has been confirmed by statistical and other studies; but it would seem that Sanderson did no more than plot on a map the location of a number of air and sea disasters, concluding that those places where there had been a large number of losses were 'vile vortices'. This is about as valid as suggesting that a major motorway is a 'vile vortex' because more accidents happen there than on a remote country lane.

One such 'vile vortex', called the Devil's Sea, lies off the coast of Japan, but precisely where off the coast of Japan is something that few writers agree about. For Charles Berlitz and Vincent Gaddis it is south or south-east of Japan, between Japan and the Bonin Islands; John Godwin places it between Iwo Jima and Marcus Island; Adi-Kent Thomas Jeffrey and John Wallace Spencer put it between Japan and the Marianas; Ivan T. Sanderson locates it 250 miles (400 kilometres) south of Honshu, at about 140 degrees longitude. For Elizabeth Nichols the Devil's Sea is a triangle connecting Japan, Wake Island and Guam; for Richard Winer it is a triangle bounded by the south-east coast of Japan, the north-eastern tip of the Philippines, and Guam.

Nine large coastal freighters are said to have inexplicably vanished in the Devil's Sea between 1950 and 1954. According to Charles Berlitz the authorities undertook an 'investigation of the area in 1955. This expedition, with scientists taking data as their ship, the *Kaiyo Maru No. 5*, cruised the Devil's Sea, ended on a rather spectacular note – the survey ship suddenly vanished.' The truth of the matter is that nine fishing boats of between 62 and 192 tonnes disappeared in a 750-mile (1200-kilometre) stretch of sea between 1949 and 1953. The *Kaiyo Maru No. 5* disappeared in 1952, not in 1955, while observing the birth of an island thrust up from the sea bed by volcanic activity. The Japanese authorities have declared the region an official danger zone.

Evil doings in Atlantis?

Numerous theories have been advanced to explain the allegedly inexplicable disappearances; these range from the almost obligatory UFOs to science fiction concepts such as time travel and parallel worlds. Berlitz is of the opinion that Atlantis has been found off the coast of Bimini in the Bahamas. In the Triangle legend Atlantis is seen as the home of an antediluvian super-race, one of whose machines or weapons is still functioning somewhere on the sea bed and causing ships and aircraft to disintegrate. The earliest mention of Atlantis is to be found in an unfinished work by the Greek philosopher Plato. Plato was concerned with concepts, not history, and could weave fact with fiction without any qualms about accuracy. We have no idea whether Plato invented Atlantis or was drawing on ancient traditions, but whether or not Atlantis ever existed Plato gives no reasons for us to believe that it was a technological society. According to Plato the Atlanteans were defeated in war by the ancient Greeks.

Perhaps the most popular theory is that some kind of magnetic anomaly is causing the disappearances. Many writers point out that in the Bermuda Triangle the compass needle points to the North Pole and not to the magnetic North Pole as it does everywhere else in the world. This is not strictly true. At certain places in the world the actual North Pole and the magnetic North Pole are in a straight line, the Agonic Line, and one of those places just happens to be off the coast of Florida. As you move away from the Agonic Line so the difference in the distance between the North and magnetic North becomes greater. There is absolutely nothing mysterious about the Agonic Line. Accounts that mention compass needles gyrating wildly or otherwise acting strangely prove nothing either. Local magnetic variations can cause such behaviour and exist all over the world.

In his book *Secrets of the Bermuda Triangle* Alan Landsberg writes:

It is clear that whatever critics in the various narrow branches of science may say, something strange is unquestionably happening in the Bermuda Triangle. The world-wide interest is itself phenomenal as if the vast majority of people 'know' that there is

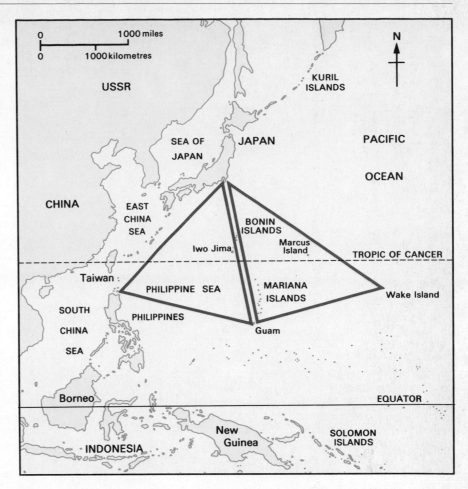

Above: the so-called Devil's Sea is one of Ivan T. Sanderson's 12 'vile vortices', areas of the globe where vanishings are said to be more frequent than elsewhere. But the location of the region is far from certain – except that it is off the coast of Japan. For Elizabeth Nichols the Devil's Sea extends eastwards to Wake Island; for Richard Winer it reaches west as far as the Philippines

Left: the *Revonoc*, a prize-winning racing yawl owned by American millionaire publisher Harvey Conover, disappeared during a trip from Key West to Miami in January 1958. Conover, his wife and two children were aboard. The Coast Guard reported that the 45-foot (14-metre) yacht had apparently been caught by near-hurricane winds in what was said to be one of the worst storms in the history of Florida

something important to be discovered there.

In effect Landsberg is invalidating expert scientific opinion by suggesting that from their position as specialists the scientific fraternity cannot take a comprehensive view of the problem. He claims to be in a far better position to comment on the Bermuda Triangle than is a scientist, because not being a scientist he is not hidebound. However, it is not critics in the narrow branches of science but the facts themselves that suggest that it is highly questionable that anything remotely strange is happening in the Triangle.

Writers about the Bermuda Triangle have a vested interest in the 'mystery' because that sells their books and earns them their money. They therefore employ many techniques to imply that a mystery exists. A great favourite is the 'as if' ploy, a minor example of which is used by Landsberg in the above quote. Charles Berlitz, perhaps the best-known of the Triangle authors, writes of how 'boats have disappeared without leaving wreckage, as if they and their crews had been snatched by another dimension'.

'Not yet' is another popular ploy. 'Scientists have not yet discovered the nature of the strange forces in the Bermuda Triangle,' which implies that scientists believe that strange forces do exist in the Triangle and are trying to find out what they are.

Sometimes Berlitz makes absurd comparisons. In *Without a trace* he says:

It has been suggested that vessels have sometimes been run down by other ships without the larger ship noticing. It was supposed that the *Revonoc* had been run over by an ocean-going freighter at night. However applicable this theory might be to sailing vessels, it would still not explain the disappearance of freighters which, if run over by other freighters, would undoubtedly be noticed.

The point here is that the theory was not intended to apply to freighters, but by connecting the two Berlitz has tried to devalue a perfectly acceptable theory for the loss of small vessels like the yacht *Revonoc*, even though the *Revonoc* disappeared in 1958 in what the *New York Times* described as 'near hurricane winds from the worst midwinter storm in the history of south Florida'.

Contrasting techniques

The jaw really does drop with disbelief when Berlitz discusses Lawrence David Kusche whose book, *The Bermuda Triangle mystery – solved*, is a crushing exposé of 50 celebrated Triangle cases. Berlitz writes that Kusche's 'approach to the subject is not influenced by any personal familiarity with the area of the Bermuda Triangle. His research techniques are characterised by a somewhat touching reliance on long-distance telephone calls as a means of investigation.' Berlitz also quotes Kusche as having said that there was nothing to be gained by going to the area to conduct research, a view that Berlitz thinks is 'a refreshing comment on investigative techniques which would immeasurably simplify the work of detectives, police, research investigators, and explorers throughout the world'. This is the extent of Berlitz's reply to Kusche's detailed criticism.

Kusche examined accident investigation reports, contemporary newspaper accounts, weather records, official documents and a wealth of important information obtained throughout the world as a result of letters and long-distance telephone calls. On the other

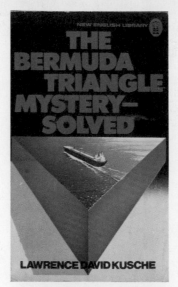

Top and above: in *The Bermuda Triangle mystery – solved* Lawrence David Kusche exposed serious factual errors in usual accounts of Bermuda Triangle disappearances

Below: the *Star Tiger* went missing in January 1948. An official enquiry remarked that 'no more baffling problem has ever been presented for investigation'

hand, had Berlitz taken the trouble to make a few telephone calls and write some letters he would not have made so many gross errors.

In *The Bermuda Triangle*, during his discussion of the disappearances of the British airliner *Star Tiger* in January 1948, Berlitz says that the last message sent by the aircraft was 'Weather and performance excellent. Expect to arrive on schedule.' No such message was ever sent at any time during the flight. The facts were fully presented in the accident investigation report (published as a government White Paper) and in press reports of the public enquiry into the matter. *Great mysteries of the air* by Ralph Barker, a book Berlitz listed in his bibliography, contains a chapter about the *Star Tiger* from which it is clear that the weather was bad when the plane went missing. Kusche's *The Bermuda Triangle mystery – solved* gives the facts again, but although Berlitz presumably read it (because he criticised its author) he repeated the 'Weather and performance excellent' story in his later book *Without a trace*.

The Bermuda Triangle is a manufactured mystery. Many readers who do not wish to believe this will argue that there is no smoke without fire. And articles critical of the alleged Triangle mysteries always provoke accusations that the author has a closed mind or is merely a professional debunker. In the introduction to her book *They dared the devil's triangle*, Adi-Kent Thomas Jeffrey implores her readers:

Let us not cover our senses with the impenetrable armour of suspicion and scepticism. Let us not don the thick helmet of closed-mindedness under the guise of so-called 'common sense' and 'reason'.

But who is being closed-minded? There is probably a great deal still to be learned about our world and the Universe in which we live, and study of unexplained phenomena may one day lead to new and exciting discoveries. But extraordinary and alarming claims for unknown forces causing the loss of ships and aircraft *must* be backed by hard, incontrovertible facts. This is not the case with the Bermuda Triangle.

As far as can be ascertained, not one of the Triangle authors has satisfactorily replied to the critics. And they have never said where certain documents can be found, or where it says that the last message from the *Star Tiger* was 'Weather and performance excellent', or why they believe the *Bella* and *Freya* were Triangle fatalities, or why the *Atalanta*, *Anglo-Australian*, *Connemara IV*, *Sandra*, *Revonoc*, and the rest were not victims of storms and hurricanes. Until they do, it is the Bermuda Triangle writers who have closed minds, not their critics.

Whatever happened to Flight 19?

The case of Flight 19 sums up the whole Bermuda Triangle myth. Triangle writers have made much of the story of the missing bombers but the popularised tale lacked one ingredient – the facts

THE DISAPPEARANCE OF FLIGHT 19 – five US Navy bombers that vanished over the Bermuda Triangle in 1945 – is the central element of the Bermuda Triangle myth. The opening sequence of the film *Close encounters of the third kind* (1977) has the aircraft being discovered, over 30 years after the disappearance, in the desert of northern Mexico, thus turning fact into fiction – or to be more accurate, turning fiction that had been made into fact back into fiction again, because the story of Flight 19 is one of the most distorted stories in the whole Bermuda Triangle myth.

According to the Triangle version of the story, the five Grumman TBM Avenger

Five US Navy bombers of the same type as Flight 19. Did it really disappear under mysterious circumstances in the Bermuda Triangle, or is there a more prosaic explanation for the tragedy?

bombers left the runway at the Naval Air Station, Fort Lauderdale, Florida, at 2 p.m. on 5 December 1945. Charles Berlitz says that the aircraft were 'on a routine training mission . . . both pilots and crews were experienced airmen'. Berlitz says that 'pilots who had flown earlier the same day reported ideal flying weather.'

At 3.45 p.m. the flight leader, Lieutenant Charles C. Taylor, radioed the control tower. 'Calling tower. This is an emergency. We seem to be off course. We cannot see land . . . repeat . . . we cannot see land.'

'What is your position?' radioed the tower.

'We're not sure of our position. We cannot be sure just where we are. We seem to be lost.'

'Assume bearing due west.'

'We don't know which way is west. Everything is wrong . . . strange. We can't be sure of just where we are. We are not sure of any direction. Even the ocean doesn't look as it should.'

Lieutenant Robert Cox, senior flight instructor at Fort Lauderdale, had been preparing to land when he overheard these messages and he thought he knew where Flight 19 was. He radioed, 'Flight 19, what is your altitude? I'll fly south and meet you.'

Taylor should have welcomed any assistance, but for a few minutes he was silent

before he cried, 'Don't come after me! They look like. . . .'

Silence. The time was now 4.30 p.m. As the last message from Flight 19 was being received a huge Martin Mariner sea plane, dispatched on a rescue mission, was nearing the bombers' last estimated position. It sent one message and then followed the bombers into oblivion. Six military aircraft had vanished in the space of a few hours!

There followed one of the largest air-sea searches in history, but not a single scrap of wreckage or debris was found. There were no survivors. Investigators were completely baffled. At the end of the long enquiry one Navy officer commented that Flight 19 and the sea plane had 'vanished as completely as if they had flown to Mars'.

To compound the mystery there is the vexing question of why Lieutenant Taylor refused help from Cox. And what did Taylor see when he cried 'They look like. . . .'? Joan Powers, widow of one of Flight 19's crew, is quoted as saying:

My own theory is that the men saw something up there over the Triangle . . . something which so frightened Lieutenant Taylor that he did not want Lieutenant Cox to jeopardise his own life; something which, possibly for national security reasons, the Navy still does not want the public to know about.

If the Bermuda Triangle version of this disappearance is correct then the case of Flight 19 must rank as the most baffling mystery in the history of aviation. But from the official report and other reliable sources it is possible to reconstruct the events of that December day and show that the Triangle account is grossly inaccurate.

The Triangle account gives the distinct

Above: Fort Lauderdale, the US Naval Air Station in Florida from where the ill-fated Flight 19 took off at 2 p.m. on 5 December 1945

Below: Lieutenant Robert Cox, senior flight instructor at Fort Lauderdale in 1945, who received the controversial last radio message from Flight 19

impression of cloudless skies and a group of experienced airmen flying a route they knew like the back of their hands; but although the weather was fine when the aircraft left Fort Lauderdale it rapidly deteriorated during the flight, and search craft later reported unsafe flying conditions and tremendous seas. With the exception of Lieutenant Taylor none of the crew was highly experienced. They had only about 300 flying hours each, only 60 of which were in TBM-type aircraft. Taylor, a combat veteran with 2509 flying hours, had recently moved to Fort Lauderdale from Miami, was unfamiliar with the area, and had never before flown the route taken by Flight 19. The flight was 'routine' only in the sense that it was an established training exercise at Fort Lauderdale. It was, in fact, a complicated navigation exercise.

The undiscover'd country

The first message from the aircraft was not received by the Fort Lauderdale tower but by Lieutenant Cox, who overheard an inter-aircraft communication in which somebody asked Captain Edward Powers what his compass read. 'I don't know where we are,' replied Powers. 'We must have got lost after that last turn.'

Lieutenant Cox radioed, 'What is your trouble?'

Taylor replied, 'Both my compasses are out. I'm trying to find Fort Lauderdale. I'm over land but it's broken. I'm sure I'm in the Keys, but I don't know how far down. . . .'

These initial communications provide the clue to Flight 19's ultimate fate. Lieutenant Taylor and, apparently, Captain Powers, the next most experienced man among the crew, believed that Flight 19 had taken a wrong turn and flown off course. The aircraft were over Great Sale Cay in the Bahamas, but Lieutenant Taylor, who had never flown over the area, was struck by the similarity between Great Sale Cay and the Florida

Keys, with which he was very familiar, having flown over them many times while stationed at Miami. Taylor could not decide whether he was to the east or west of the Florida Peninsula – over the Atlantic Ocean or the Gulf of Mexico.

Lieutenant Cox gave Taylor instructions for reaching Fort Lauderdale from the Keys and added, 'What is your altitude? I'll fly south and meet you.'

This is a statement that Triangle writers make much of, but the official report says that Taylor replied, 'I know where I am now. I'm at 2300 feet [700 metres]. Don't come after me.' There is no mention of anything looking remotely unusual.

Taylor did not know where he was, however, and he became increasingly disorientated. Many factors contributed to his disorientation: his compasses were not working, or he believed they weren't; he didn't have a clock or watch; his radio channel was subject to interference from Cuban radio stations, but the fear of losing contact with the flight deterred him from changing frequencies to the undisturbed emergency channel.

In the gathering dusk he led the aircraft first in one direction, then in another, and as dusk was replaced by the black darkness of a winter's night, the weather and the sea grew rough. At 6.30 p.m. Lieutenant Taylor, valiantly trying to keep his flight together, was heard to announce: 'All planes close up tight . . . we will have to ditch unless landfall . . . when the first plane drops to 10 gallons [45 litres] we all go down together.'

The last words heard from any of the aircraft were at 7.04 p.m. when one of the pilots was heard trying to contact Lieutenant Taylor. It is assumed that some time during the next hour the five bombers descended

A Martin Mariner sea plane of the type that set off to try to locate Flight 19 – and also apparently vanished. It left the Banana River Naval Air Station (now Patrick Air Force Base) at 7.30 p.m. and is believed to have exploded in mid-air a short time afterwards. The captain of the freighter *Gaines Mills* reported seeing an aircraft burst into flames and explode, and the commander of the USS *Solomons* confirmed that the Mariner disappeared from its radar screen at about the same time as the *Gaines Mills* saw the explosion. Yet strangely, Triangle writers persist in describing the Mariner's fate as a 'mysterious disappearance'

through the night to the turbulent sea below. Experts later testified that a TBM would sink in less than a minute.

An air search was launched almost immediately but was little more than a token gesture because the chances of spotting wreckage at night and in bad weather were slim. By daylight the sea would have dispersed wreckage beyond recognition.

The Triangle version of Flight 19 presents a set of wholly spurious radio messages and has the aircraft vanishing some two and a half hours earlier than was probably the case. As for the rescue aircraft that followed the bombers into oblivion it must be considered a separate incident.

Fire in the sky

Some books have the Martin Mariner sea plane vanishing some three hours before it had even taken off. In fact, the aircraft left the Banana River naval airfield (now Patrick Air Force Base) at 7.30 p.m., sent a routine departure message and is believed to have exploded in mid-air a short time later. Charles Berlitz refers to this explanation in his book *Without a trace*: 'The vanishing Martin Mariner,' he says, 'is conveniently explained by the fact that a flare in the night sky was observed by the crew of the *Gaines Mills*, a passing freighter.' What Berlitz considers to be a flare in the night sky was described somewhat differently by the captain of the *Gaines Mills* who reported seeing an aircraft catch fire, plummet into the sea and explode.

The commander of the USS *Solomons*, an aircraft carrier participating in the search, confirmed that it was the sea plane that had exploded. The aircraft was tracked on the *Solomons*'s air search radar from the time it left Banana River until it vanished from the screen at the same time and in the same location as the *Gaines Mills* had observed an explosion.

Nobody knows what caused the explosion, but Mariners were labelled 'flying gas

tanks' and they carried a large quantity of high-octane fuel. The fumes that gathered inside the hull could have been ignited by a spark generated by anything from an electrical fault to pieces of metal rubbing against each other.

The only mystery about Flight 19 that remains to be solved is the origin of the messages supposed to have passed between Lieutenant Taylor and the Lauderdale tower. Their earliest appearance in print is an article by Allan W. Eckert published in 1962. Eckert cannot remember his source. Charles Berlitz says that much of his information about Flight 19 came from the first-hand notes made by Commander R. H. Wirshing, then lieutenant on duty at Fort Lauderdale, but in a BBC television documentary about the Bermuda Triangle Commander Wirshing denied that he had kept firsthand notes and said that he did not arrive on duty until Flight 19 could no longer receive messages from the tower.

The case of Flight 19 is typical of the entire Bermuda Triangle myth. Facts have been distorted, there are gross errors and twisted and distorted details. It is a manufactured mystery that has developed over 40 years as one writer has taken his information from another, elaborating bits here and there, doing little original research, and perpetuating errors – each believing that his information has already been verified by somebody else. And so it goes on.

Above: the USS *Solomons*, the aircraft carrier that searched for the lost Martin Mariner – and reported its explosion

Right: map showing the Florida Keys (A), with which Lieutenant Taylor, leader of Flight 19, was familiar. He mistook Great Sale Cay (B), over which he was flying, for the Keys and became increasingly disorientated shortly before losing radio contact with ground control and presumably crashing

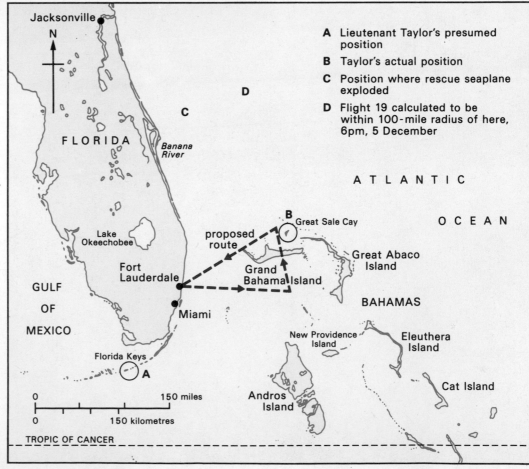

A Lieutenant Taylor's presumed position

B Taylor's actual position

C Position where rescue seaplane exploded

D Flight 19 calculated to be within 100-mile radius of here, 6pm, 5 December

Out of thin air

Murdered men with no traceable past; navigators of medieval 'cloud-ships'; mermen – PAUL BEGG discusses these, and others, who have suddenly appeared to disrupt our comfortable and ordered view of reality

THE FAINT HEARTS of some genteel young ladies hurrying about their business in the High Street, Chatham, Kent, received something of a shock on 6 January 1914. A naked man suddenly appeared in their midst and began running up and down the road. Nobody had seen a naked man in the area surrounding the High Street. Nobody had seen a man undress. The man's clothes were searched for, but could not be found. Finer sensibilities were saved from further offence when a policeman caught the man and took him to the police station. The man could tell nothing about himself and was eventually declared insane.

West Botley flyover near Oxford, England. A man was found dead – apparently having fallen from the flyover. The corpse eluded identification; the only clues were five handkerchiefs, bearing the letter 'M' – and a strip of foil containing 15 tablets of a drug that was so new that few doctors even knew it existed

In 1851, a man was found wandering in a village near Frankfurt-an-der-Oder in what is now East Germany. He could not explain how he had got there, but said that he lived in Laxaria in a country called Sakria. Neither place was or is now known to exist.

In 1975, a man in a neatly pressed pinstripe suit was found dead, apparently having fallen from the West Botley flyover near Oxford. The manufacturers' labels had been removed from his clothes and the body bore no identification. The man carried five handkerchiefs, each of which bore the initial 'M', and a thin strip of foil containing 15 tablets of a new drug called Vivalan. The drug was so new that few doctors knew of its existence and those who did had prescribed it only to women, none of whom knew who 'M' was. The identity of the man has remained a mystery. 'M', it seems, had stepped out of thin air – presumably at some point above the A420 road – and plummeted to his death.

One day in September 1877, Mr W. H. Smith glanced at the sky over Brooklyn, New York City. He had never before seen anything in the sky except clouds, birds, and snowflakes in winter, and he probably did not expect to see anything different when he glanced heavenward on that particular day. In fact he saw 'a winged human form' and the sight so impressed and startled him that he wrote a letter to the *New York Sun* about it.

On 12 October 1976, eight-year-old Tonnlie Barefoot of Dunn, North Carolina,

linked to but separate from our own. As Evans Wentz put it in his *The fairy faith in Celtic countries* (1909): 'There never seems to have been an uncivilized tribe, a race or nation of civilized men, who have not had some form of belief in an unseen world, peopled by unseen beings.'

In the ninth century, St Agobard, Archbishop of Lyons in France, wrote in his *Liber de Grandine at Tonitruis*:

We have seen and heard many who are overwhelmed by such madness, carried away by such folly, that they believe and assert that there is a certain region called Magonia (The Magic Land), whence ships come in the clouds. . . . Certain folk have we seen, blinded by so dark a folly, who brought into an assembly four persons, three men and a woman, as having fallen from the said ships; whom they had held in bonds for certain days and then presented them before an assembled body of men, in our presence, as aforesaid, in order that they should be stoned. Howbeit, the truth prevailed, after much reasoning, and they who brought them forward were confounded.

Enemy agents

What seems to have happened is that three men and a woman were seen or were said to have been seen descending from a 'cloud-ship'. A crowd gathered and became furious when somebody claimed that the strangers were the agents of an enemy of Charlemagne and had come to destroy the crops. The four people tried in vain to vindicate themselves, saying that they were ordinary people who had until recently lived near Lyons, but that they had been taken away by men who could work miracles and who had shown them marvellous things. The peasants did not believe one word of this and were about to

saw a little man 'not much bigger than a Coke bottle' who wore black boots, blue trousers and a blue top with 'the prettiest little white tie you ever saw'. The boy insisted that he had seen the little man and became very upset when his story was not believed. But disconcertingly for adult doubters, Tonnlie was able to show where he had seen the mini-man and a search revealed a clear trail of tiny footprints.

A naked man appearing from nowhere, a man from somewhere that does not exist, a tiny man with a pretty white tie, a 'thing' with wings, an unidentified corpse with a surfeit of handkerchiefs . . . For centuries reliable, sober people have been reporting encounters with people, creatures and 'weird things' that cannot be identified and in some cases seem beyond identification. In one sense it does not matter if the cited examples of these reports are true or capable of a rational explanation. Their importance lies in the fact that they reflect a belief in a world

Above: the tiny footprints allegedly made by the little man 'not much bigger than a Coke bottle' seen by Tonnlie Barefoot (right) of Dunn, North Carolina, USA, in 1976. The tiny man wore, among other things, 'the prettiest little white tie you ever saw'. Not unnaturally perhaps, Tonnlie's story was greeted with some reservation by adults – until they found the footprints

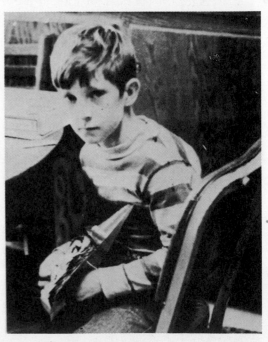

stone the four strangers when Agobard, attracted by the noise, came running to see what was going on. He listened to the opinions of both parties and then pronounced that cloud-ships did not exist, therefore the strangers could not have descended from one and were accordingly innocent of the crime of which they were accused. The peasants accepted this, which suggests that St Agobard was blessed with an enviable silver tongue, and the strangers were released to go about their business. As for Agobard, he seems to have considered the whole business to be no more than a manifestation of paganism. He wrote despairingly:

> The wretched world lies now under the tyranny of foolishness: things are believed by Christians of such absurdity as no one could aforetime induce the heathen to believe, who knew not of the creator of all.

The Magonians return

Despite Agobard's reasoning, the Magonians did not disappear but were still around 300 years later. In his *Otia Imperialia* (*c.*1211) the chronicler Gervaise of Tilbury wrote that one morning as the populace came out from mass they saw an anchor let down from a cloud-ship and accidentally become attached to a tomb. A cloud-sailor came down the rope hand over hand and freed the anchor.

> When, however, he had torn the anchor from the tomb, he was caught by those who stood around, in whose arms he gave up the ghost, stifled by the breath of our gross air even as a ship-wrecked mariner is stifled in the sea. Moreover, his fellows above, judging him to be wrecked . . . cut the cable, left their anchor, and sailed away.

Gervaise's account is even more remarkable than St Agobard's but one should beware of attaching modern interpretations to these medieval tales. In context of the period they can be less than mysterious. The Church has long been obsessed with the godlessness of mankind, and the medieval cleric was obsessed with the concept of war between the agents of God and Satan, frequently seeing evidence of the battle in the most natural of things. Nevertheless, the story is still very interesting as one of the more bizarre examples of the strange creatures that were repeatedly reported during the Middle Ages.

Writing of his own time, Gervaise makes the remarkable and perhaps startling comment that in the British Ocean (the Channel) mermaids and mermen lived in considerable number. One of the most detailed accounts of a merman is to be found in the *Chronicum Anglicarum* by Ralph of Coggeshall, a chronicler contemporary with, and possibly a friend of, Gervaise of Tilbury. Ralph writes:

> In the time of King Henry II, when Bartholomew de Glanville kept Orford Castle, it happened that the sailors there, fishing in the sea, caught a wild man in their nets. . . . He was completely naked and had the appearance of a man in all his parts. He had hair too . . . his beard was profuse and pointed, and he was exceedingly shaggy. . . .

The merman was kept under guard for several days. He eagerly ate what food was given to him, showing preference for raw fish. When taken into a church he displayed no sign of reverence or even understanding. He also insisted on sleeping when the Sun sank and waking when the Sun rose.

> He would not utter any speech, or rather he could not, even when hung up by his feet and cruelly tortured. . . . Once they took him to the sea-gate and let him go into the water, after placing a triple row of strong nets in front of him. He soon made for the deep sea, and,

Below: the 'very frightful spectacle' that greeted the citizens of Nuremberg, Germany, at sunrise on 14 April 1561. To the medieval mind the strange and inexplicable objects – and people – that suddenly confronted them were only to be expected. It is little wonder that the belief in the 'cloud-ships' that were reported in both France and England was so widespread

> breaking through the nets, raised himself again and again from the depths, and showed himself to those watching on the shore, often plunging into the sea, and a little later coming up, as if he were jeering at the spectators because he had escaped their nets.

For some reason, after the 'merman' had cavorted in the sea to his satisfaction, he returned to the shore and stayed with the folk of Orford for about two months before going once more into the sea, this time for ever.

> But whether he was mortal man, or a kind of fish bearing resemblance to humanity, or an evil spirit lurking in the body of a drowned man, such as we read of in the life of the blessed Audon, it is difficult to decide, all the more so because one hears so many remarkable things, and there is such a number of happenings like this.

The 16th-century chronicler Raphael Holinshed also mentions the Orford 'merman',

dating his appearance as 1197, the first year of the reign of King John.

Another bizarre story from the Middle Ages is that of the strange children who materialised at Woolpit in Suffolk. Their skin was green and they claimed to have come from 'St Martin's land', a place of perpetual twilight.

To the 20th-century mind these stories are outstanding examples, proof perhaps, of flying machines in the ninth century, of other worlds called Magonia and St Martin's land, and of a human being so well-adapted to the water that perhaps he could only be a descendant of the survivors of sunken Atlantis. But to the medieval mind such things were pretty tame, commonplace stuff compared to

Above: Orford Castle, Suffolk. Ralph of Coggeshall, the 13th-century chronicler, recorded that the fishermen of Orford had caught a merman (above right) in their nets. He was exceedingly shaggy, but otherwise he resembled a man. They placed him under guard and tortured him to make him speak, but he could not. He stayed with his captors for a total of two months before finally returning to his home under the sea

some of the many fabulous creatures that occupied the thoughts of the early Christian Church. In his *De Civitate Dei*, St Augustine of Hippo (345–430) wondered whether 'any monsterous kinds of men' were begotten by the sons of Adam. He tentatively concluded that the instance of abnormal birth supported the existence of creatures such as the Cyclops, another monster, which had its head in its breast, and Sciopodes, bizarre things that were able to run very swiftly despite the fact that they had only one leg, which could not bend. The single foot was so large that the creatures could use it to shade themselves from the Sun while they slept.

If the medieval mind could accept the reality of such fabulous creatures, it would

Left: some of the bizarre creatures discussed by St Augustine (345–430) in his *De Civitate Dei*: those with heads in their breasts, with only one eye and with only one foot. He concluded that these and other aberrations could be accounted for in terms of monstrous human births

have little difficulty in accepting Magonians, merfolk, and green children. And it is also interesting to note that, while the majority of the fabulous creatures described by people such as St Augustine have been relegated to the waste bin of discredited marvels, flying machines, merfolk and other almost human apparitions have continued to be seen throughout the ages.

One such well-documented story dates from 1955. On the night of Sunday, 21 August a 'little man' was seen approaching the Sutton family farmhouse near the small town of Kelly, to the north of Hopkinsville, Kentucky, USA. As the creature came to within 20 feet (6 metres) of the house, its arms raised, two of the Suttons shot at it. The creature somersaulted with the impact of the bullet, but it seemed otherwise unhurt and disappeared into the darkness. But there were more of them – and when the Suttons shot at them they, too, seem to feel no ill effects from the bullets that ricocheted off them – although they were knocked to the ground. The Suttons' hospitality to these 'little men', described as being about 3½ feet (1 metre) tall with large eyes and elephantine ears, consisted of shooting the contents of about four boxes of .22 shells at them.

Eventually the Suttons, frightened and alarmed by the creatures, abandoned their home and drove to the Hopkinsville police station, where they arrived in a state of excitement bordering on shock. Investigators later testified that the Suttons were genuinely agitated, that shots had been fired, and that no evidence of drinking had been found. The only conclusion that seemed possible was that the Sutton family really had seen what they claimed – but what was it?

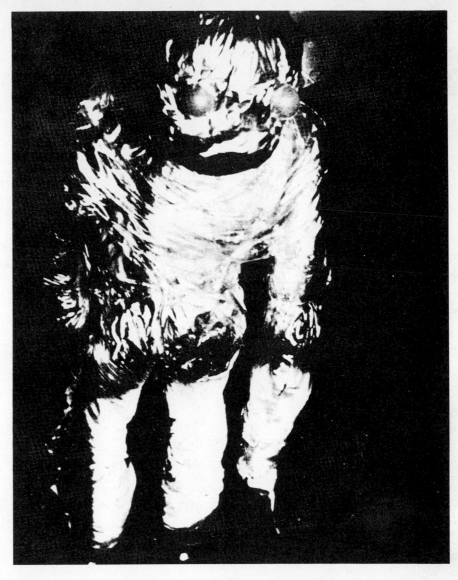

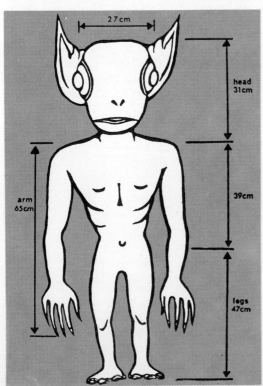

When several small goblins approached the Suttons' farm, near Hopkinsville, Kentucky, USA, on the night of 21 August 1955, they were greeted with a hail of bullets. However, the little men kept on coming, unharmed by the shooting. The Suttons panicked and drove straight to the nearest police station, where they were said to have arrived in a state of considerable shock. Later a model was made of the goblins (above) and a sketch (left) by Pauline Bowen appeared in *The humanoids* (1969). What were the goblins – creatures from another dimension? Entities from UFOs? Mass hallucinations?

It is interesting to note that strange, white, large-eyed people had previously been reported in the history of the area.

The Kelly goblin is but one of an assortment of weird and wonderful creatures that have been linked with close encounters of the third kind. But the phenomenon is much more complex than it appears at first glance. The mystery of 'appearing people', which could include ghosts and even the Loch Ness monster and the Abominable Snowman, dates as far back as written records will take us. Of course historical sightings cannot necessarily be taken as fact and more recent reports – in spite of having been made by people whose veracity we often have no reason to question – have not proved sufficiently convincing to persuade sceptics that there is a genuine phenomenon to investigate seriously. But one fact cannot be disputed; for whatever reason, thousands of people have seen, and continue to see, weird creatures that, in our reality, are not supposed to exist. Why they are seen is another question.

One-way ticket from nowhere

For centuries there have been reports of people suddenly appearing who have no known identity, or whose background is a complete mystery. Are there any explanations for these bizarre cases?

IT IS PERHAPS a telling symptom of modern society that some people can disappear and not be missed. There are dozens of accounts of people who have been found, usually dead – sometimes in strange circumstances – without any identification on their persons and without any kin or friends searching for them. While not all these people's deaths can be considered truly mysterious – at least not in the paranormal sense – sometimes the manner of their passing is so unusual that we are forced to look at the matter afresh.

For example: in November 1888 two residents of Birmingham, Alabama, USA, were murdered and their bodies were found in some woods. Nearby there was a third corpse. 'The body lies unidentified in the undertaker's rooms,' reported the *St Louis Globe Democrat*, continuing:

No one who has seen it can remember having seen the man in life, and identification seems impossible. The dead man was evidently in good circumstances, if not wealthy, and what he could have been doing at the spot where his body was found is a mystery. Several persons who have seen the body are of the opinion that the man was a foreigner. Anyway he was an entire stranger in this vicinity, and his coming must have been as mysterious as his death.

In 1920 a naked man was found in a ploughed

Corpses that yield few clues to their identity have been found even in bureaucratic modern times, when everyone seems to be well-documented. An unknown man plummeted to his death from Kestrel House, Islington, London (left), in 1975. And corpses with no past have been discovered – amid some publicity – in Petersfield, Hampshire (right), and in Yellowham Woods (far right) and on Chesil Beach (top right) in Dorset, in the 1970s

shore near Weymouth five months later; and the third was found in Yellowham Woods, near Dorchester, in March 1975. None of the men was identified.

In 1975 a young man plummeted from the 17-storey Kestrel House in City Road, Islington, London. The man, who was not wearing a jacket or overcoat, despite it being midwinter, carried no clue to his identity beyond two bus tickets issued by South-ampton Corporation and an envelope addressed to the National Savings head-quarters in Glasgow. But both these potential clues led nowhere.

Inspector Robert Gibson of King's Cross police said that he could not accept that this outwardly respectable young man could have gone missing without somebody trying to find out where he was. However, when the

Unclothed Man's Death From Exposure.

From Our Special Correspondent.

PETERSFIELD, Thursday.

Who is the blue-eyed man whose nude body was found in a ploughed field at East Meon, near here, six weeks ago?

That a man could wander near to the main road between Petersfield and Win-chester in a nude condition until he died in a field from exposure, aggravated by minor injuries such as cuts and abrasions, is astonishing, but that his identity and everything connected with his death should remain a mystery to-day is almost unbelievable. It is a baffling mystery.

The man's nails were manicured, the palms of his hands showed that he was not engaged in manual labour, and his features and general appearance were those of someone of a superior class. But although his photograph has been circu-lated north, east, south and west through the United Kingdom, the police are still without a clue, and there is no record of any missing person bearing the slightest resemblance to this man, presumably of education and good standing.

THEORIES AND SPECULATION.

There are plenty of theories. The popu-lar one, according to my information, is that the man was brought to Peak Farm in a motor-car and was turned out to stumble along the highway presumably at about midnight, and perhaps intoxicated.

The railway runs near the ploughed field. Is it possible that he was thrown or fell from a train, his clothing having first been removed? There was a tear in the palm of one hand, cuts on the soles of the feet, bruises on the wrist and legs, and scratches on the arms. Dr. Stafford, who examined the body, believes that these injuries may have been caused by strug-gling through the hedges, falling over obstacles, etc.

The Coroner suggested at the inquest that the man may have been suffering from neurasthenia or shell shock—but his relatives would surely in that event have reported his disappearance or his clothes would have been found. As some-one down here said to me: "When a tramp dies by the roadside he is generally in rags." This man certainly did not appear to be of the tramp class, and it seems incredible that he could have vanished from the world without being missed.

MYSTERIOUS MOTOR-CAR.

A police official who has been engaged on the case told me to-day that there was a trail through the coppice where the man had torn his way through. He had pushed his way through brambles that seem almost as formidable as a barbed-wire entanglement. No one but a mad-man would do such a thing.

It is possible, of course, that he was a soldier from one of the camps round here, and that he is posted as an absentee, but the inquiries have so far failed to support this suggestion.

I was told to-night of a shepherd who was watching his flocks in a field near to where the man was found, and he says that in the small hours of the morning he heard a motor-car stop and restart close by. The night was bitterly cold.

A cottager who lives not very far away also heard a car stop at about the same time.

field near Petersfield, Hampshire. Prints of the man's bare feet were traced to the road, and across the road into another field. A search of this field failed to find the man's clothing. As far as the evidence indicated, the man had appeared from nowhere, wandered aimlessly, perhaps in desperation – his body bore scratches such as would be made by bushes and hedges – until he died from exposure. That the poor fellow was un-familiar with the area is suggested by the fact that he was only a mile (1.6 kilometres) from the nearest house. A photograph of the man was widely circulated, but nobody recog-nised him. 'There is no record of any missing person bearing the slightest resemblance to this man, presumably of good education and standing,' reported the London *Daily News*.

And such unidentified corpses continue to be found. On 1 December 1975, an inquest was held in Dorchester, England, into the deaths of three men. The first had been washed up on Chesil Beach, Dorset, in March 1974; the second was found on the

story of the 'Death Plunge Man' was re-ported in the *Sunday Express*, his body had been unidentified for a year. Said Inspector Gibson: 'Somebody somewhere must have loved him or at least known him.' Perhaps they did, but perhaps the 'somewhere' where they were was not the same 'somewhere' where we are.

These are just a few of the hundreds of examples of the unidentified and mysterious dead. Most of them can probably be ex-plained by the fact that we live in a relatively rootless society where people easily move from place to place and can die hundreds or thousands of miles from home and friends. But this convenient idea certainly does not explain all peculiar appearances of dead men.

There are also numerous cases of so-called 'wild people' – not to be confused with people raised by animals, such as Romulus and Remus – who seem to have entered our world as if from another dimension. They are frequently unable to account for themselves and they can at best be described as total

amnesiacs. Some may subsequently be identified, but since the media soon lose interest and rarely pursue such cases it is often difficult to discover the outcome and ultimate fate of the appearer. A few, however, have become celebrities – the mysterious Count St Germain, for example, and Kaspar Hauser, who is perhaps the most famous 'appearing person' who ever lived. Kaspar was found wandering in Nuremberg in 1828, unable to say anything about himself or about how he had got there. But Kaspar was not a simple amnesiac. He said that for as long as he could remember he had been confined in a small, dimly lit room and had never seen the face of his captor. Who had held Kaspar Hauser captive, and why, has remained a mystery.

Royalty calls

Remarkable though it is, the story of Kaspar is by no means unique. Equally complex is the story of Princess Caraboo. On the evening of 3 April 1817, a girl knocked on the door of a cottage near Bristol and in an unknown language asked for food (although how the residents of the cottage knew that she was asking for food if she spoke an unknown language is as yet an unanswered question). The girl ended up standing before a magistrate, Samuel Worrell, who took her to his home. The girl's language and her equally unrecognisable writing attracted linguists from around the country, but none could understand what she was saying until one, Manuel Eyenesso, said that she was speaking in the Malay language. She was, he said, Princess Caraboo and she had been

Above left: Kaspar Hauser, perhaps the most famous of all 'appearing persons'. His strange tale of imprisonment, and the bizarre manner of his death – he was apparently murdered by an assailant who was himself a mystery – added to the enduring interest of his story

Above: a *woodwose*, one of the wild men believed to inhabit woodland Britain. There have been many reports of such people being caught by villagers, but the wild men spoke no intelligible language – which only added to the conundrum

Right: 'The Wonder of the West', or 'Princess Caraboo', who appeared at the door of an English cottage in 1817. She spoke a strange language, which was eventually identified as Malayan. However, an ordinary Englishwoman claimed her as her daughter. The truth about 'Princess Caraboo' remains obscure

kidnapped by pirates from her home in Java. After many adventures she had managed to escape from them and eventually reached England.

However, a Mrs Willcocks then arrived from the village of Witheridge in Devon and said that Princess Caraboo was her daughter Mary. Mary confessed to the deception and was entrusted to the care of Mrs Willcocks, who sent her to America, where she disappeared from the public gaze. So what of Manuel Eyenesso's fabulous story? He, it seems, was an impostor who 'translated' Mary's gibberish into a story of his own invention. Thus we have two impostors for the price of one. Or do we?

Sources differ to a considerable extent. According to one, Mrs Worrell (the wife of the magistrate) had gone to Witheridge and there located Mrs Willcocks and established Mary's identity. Moreover, it was Mrs Worrell who paid for the girl to go to America and, once there, Mary (or Princess Caraboo) did not disappear but gave exhibitions, in Philadelphia and elsewhere, of her unknown writing.

We are left, then, with two irreconcilable stories and at least two impostors. If Princess Caraboo was really Mary Willcocks, then Manuel Eyenesso must have been an impostor because he declared that she was speaking Malay, which was highly unlikely. Again, it was Eyenesso who said she was Princess Caraboo. And we have Mrs Willcocks who, if Princess Caraboo and Eyenesso were genuine, was not the mother of Mary and was therefore an impostor. And there is Mrs Worrell who, though not an impostor, may have concocted the whole Mary story simply to get the girl away from Mrs Worrell's

The Wonder of the West.

"And where did she come from? and who can she be?
Did she fall from the sky? did she rise from the sea?"

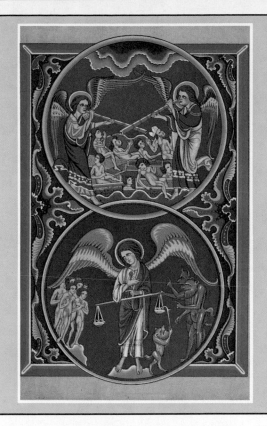

With a pinch of salt

The Bible offers many stories of mysterious 'appearing people', who are more generally known as angels. They are not always winged or bathed in a heavenly golden glow, nor do they always appear in dreams. On the contrary, they often seem solidly human in every respect. For example, take the angels who came to Abraham as he was sitting 'in the tent door in the heat of the day' and told him that his aged wife Sarah would bear a child (Genesis 18). The three angels looked like men and they behaved like men – even dining with Abraham.

Similarly the two angels who came to Lot and told him to gather his family and flee from Sodom (Genesis 19) were clearly of human form, and are repeatedly referred to as 'men'. Again, we are told that they ate, rested and took shelter with Lot, yet they were possessed of advance knowledge of the cataclysm that was about to befall the Cities of the Plain. But Lot's wife did not heed their advice not to look back on the destruction – and she was turned into a pillar of salt, which was left standing in the desert.

husband. The permutations of the Caraboo story leave the brain in a whirl.

Five 'wild men' and a 'wild girl' were found in Connecticut, USA, in January 1888. Between 1904 and 1905 ten 'wild men' were found in various parts of England. One of them is reported to have spoken a language that nobody had heard before and to have carried a book in which there was unknown and unidentified writing. Between 1920 and

Below: the High Street, Chatham, Kent, where a bewildered naked man was found wandering on 6 January 1914. He could give no account of himself and was finally declared insane and locked up in the Medway Infirmary for the rest of his life

1923 six people were found wandering in or near Romford, Essex. None could say how they had got there or tell anything about themselves.

In 1923 a naked man was seen several times at Lord Carnarvon's country estate near Newbury, Hampshire. By a striking coincidence he was first seen on 17 March, the day on which Lord Carnarvon fell ill, and was last seen on 5 April, the day Carnarvon died.

There is also the story of the naked man who, in the afternoon of Tuesday 6 January 1914, suddenly appeared in the High Street, Chatham, Kent (see page 23). The man's identity was not established and he was later declared insane and taken to Medway Infirmary.

Charles Fort, the great American collector of reports of strange happenings, commented on the Chatham naked man in his book *Lo!*:

> I suspect that many persons have been put away, as insane, simply because they were gifted with uncommon insights, or had been through uncommon experiences. . . . If there have ever been instances of teleportations of human beings from somewhere else to this Earth, an examination of inmates of infirmaries and workhouses and asylums might lead to some marvelous astronomical disclosures. . . . Early in the year 1928 a man did appear in a town in New Jersey, and did tell that he had come from the planet Mars. Wherever he came from, everybody knows where he went, after telling that.

Into thin air

People, animals and ordinary household objects that vanish into thin air or appear suddenly in unlikely places – these have always been part of folklore. But, as LYNN PICKNETT points out, the disappearances continue . . .

Right: Benjamin Bathurst, a Foreign Office employee, who disappeared in Berlin in 1809

Below: pigs, sheep and heifers were the victims of a series of disappearances from a farm near Manchester in 1974

'NOW YOU SEE HER, now you don't.' So runs the stage illusionist's traditional patter as he makes his assistant disappear. It's a skilful and enjoyable trick, this disappearing act – but even in the everyday world, far from the stage door, there have been many disappearances and strange reappearances. Only for a handful of them are there rational explanations; most of them are so extraordinary that they almost defy belief.

On 29 November 1809 Benjamin Bathurst, an employee of the British Foreign Office, was about to board a coach outside an inn near Berlin. He went to look at the horses and vanished forever.

In June 1900, Sherman Church ran into a cotton mill at Augusta Mills near Lake Michigan, USA. He never came out and could not be found again.

In 1974 pigs, sheep and heifers vanished from two farms near Manchester, England.

Weird and apparently random phenomena such as these were the province of Charles Hoy Fort, an American who published his *Book of the damned* in 1919. This – his most famous book – is a collection of well-attested stories, with a few sly hints that the natural world is one huge practical joke expressed through rains of frogs, people who disappear into nothing and people who come from nowhere. Charles Fort coined the word *teleportation* to describe the forcible removal of a person or object from one place – or even plane of existence – to another by agencies unknown and unseen. According to taste, these forces have been ascribed to God, the Devil, spirit guides, fairies and UFOs.

Sister Mary's missionary flights

Sometimes the teleportee seems to be actually in two places at once – this phenomenon is called *bilocation*. A famous case of bilocation occurred in 1620 when a young nun, Sister Mary of Agreda in Spain, embarrassed her superiors with her persistent tales of her missionary 'flights' to the Jumano Indians in Mexico; she claimed she regularly made the 2000-mile (3200-kilometre) journey. No one was prepared to take her seriously, especially as she was not missed at the convent at Agreda and she made the far-fetched claim that, during her 'flight', she noticed that the earth was round. . . . Yet the official Papal missionary assigned to the Jumano, Father Alonzo de Benevides, complained to the Pope in 1622 that the Indians had already been taught about the Catholic faith by a mysterious 'lady in blue' who had handed out rosaries, crucifixes and even a chalice – which proved to be from the convent in Agreda.

On being closely questioned by Father Benevides, Sister Mary revealed a detailed knowledge of the Indians' way of life and language and described individual members of the tribe accurately.

Like most teleportation stories, that of Sister Mary and her missionary activities seems to defy classification and analysis. The fact that she 'saw' that the earth was round indicates some kind of astral travel, yet the chalice was solid enough.

The sudden appearance of solid objects, often in sealed rooms, is called *apportation*. Apports can be literally anything, from stones or musical instruments to a dish of hot food or fresh flowers out of season.

Things that go bump . . .
Apportation seems to be a favourite diversion of poltergeists, or so-called mischievous spirits; disturbed houses often provide the setting for spectacular apports appearing from thin air. Hans Bender, Director of the Institut für Grenzgebiete der Psychologie und Psychohygiene (Institute for Border Areas of Psi) in Freiburg, West Germany, has this to say of experiences of 'things that go bump in the night':

Stones, for instance, come into a closed room from outside a house during poltergeist attacks. Witnesses describe the stones falling from about 5 or 6 inches [12 or 15 centimetres] from the ceiling. They don't bounce, and when you touch them they are usually warm.

In one case . . . in Bavaria in 1969, stones came into a closed kitchen and objects flew out of the locked house. Some little dolls came out of a closed cupboard, seemingly through the very fabric of the door, and the people saw small bottles – perfume and medicine bottles – coming from the roof of the house. Interestingly, when the bottles were seen coming from the house, they were not falling in a straight line, but in a zigzag fashion, as if they were being transported, not as if they were falling free.

This notion of apports being *carried* by an invisible force accords perfectly with the spiritualists' belief that solid objects can be dematerialised and materialised through the agency of spirits. One 'spirit guide' named White Hawk described how he does it: 'I can only explain it by saying that I speed up the atomic vibrations until the stones [or other apport] are disintegrated. Then they are brought here and I slow down the vibrations until they become solid again.'

Spiritualists often explain the inability of most mortals to see the 'other side' – which is said to interpenetrate our world in space and time – by pointing out that the material world is 'dense matter', which vibrates slowly; the spiritual plane is 'refined matter', vibrating too fast for our physical perceptions. A sudden change in atomic vibration removes objects – or people – from one plane to another or one place to another, rather like the 'beaming up' and 'beaming down' of the personnel of *Star Trek*'s starship *Enterprise*.

Vanishing people have always been part of the world's folklore – fairies, giants, spirits and, recently, UFOs have allegedly abducted

Below: Sister Mary of Agreda, who made her alleged missionary 'flights' to convert the Jumano Indians of Mexico in 1620. When the first official papal missionary visited the Jumano in 1622, he found that they had already been taught about Christianity – by a mysterious 'lady in blue'. Yet Sister Mary's fellow nuns in Agreda, Spain, testified that she had not left the convent during the time that she claimed to have been in Mexico

Bottom: Dr Hans Bender, Director of the Institute for Border Areas of Psi in Freiburg in Breisgau, West Germany. Dr Bender has made a special study of objects and people that mysteriously appear and disappear

hundreds, perhaps thousands, of people. Fairies were infamous for their trick of abducting healthy babies and leaving weak 'changelings' behind instead, and various demons of legend have been blamed for removing folk from 'before the very eyes' of their friends.

But some unfortunate people disappear without any apparent supernormal agency. These random and pointless disappearances fascinated Fort, who collected a formidable dossier of them. The victims are often typical 'men in the street', uninterested in the paranormal, on whom some practical joke seems to have been played.

The 'joke' was distinctly unfunny for a man in 1655 who was going about his business in Goa, India, when he suddenly found himself back in his birthplace, Portugal. This abrupt return home was witnessed by enough people to ensure it came to the ears of the Inquisition, who naturally – for them – assumed he was a practising sorcerer. He was tried and burnt at the stake.

In Connecticut, in January 1888, passers-by were astonished by the sudden materialisation of six people in the street. All six were suffering from concussion.

The magician vanishes
Perhaps the most ironical dematerialisation was that of the stage magician, William Neff, as related by his friend L. J. Knebel, the American broadcaster. This extraordinary happening took place at the Paramount Theatre, in New York. There were few people in the audience and Neff went into his magician's patter routinely. His friend Knebel heard none of it: he was transfixed by the gradual dematerialisation of the artist. Neff became so translucent that the stage curtains could be seen through him. Curiously, the magician seemed to be unaware of his nebulous state and continued with his patter. Gradually he became solid again, beginning with a vague outline. Confronted by Knebel with this amazing occurrence, Neff confessed it was nothing whatever to do with his act! However, he was no stranger to the phenomenon – he had once partially dematerialised during his act at Chicago, and once, 'casually', in front of his very shaken wife. One supposes that if he ever learned how to reproduce this freak happening at will, he would have become a very rich man.

Someone whose fate and fortune seem inextricably linked is the Israeli sensitive, Uri Geller. Although – as far as we know – not a teleportee, his very presence in a house provokes a flurry of apports.

Professor John Hasted, head of the department of physics at Birkbeck College, University of London, set up a test to see if the young Israeli could in any way alter the structure of a vanadium carbide crystal – chosen for its particular hardness and its rarity. It was laid on a piece of metal and enclosed in a cellulose capsule. First the professor interposed his hand between Geller and the crystal. Then as witnesses watched, Geller moved his hand, and the crystal jumped twice, 'like a jumping bean'. Apparently this was all Geller had intended to do, because Professor Hasted says 'Geller stopped concentrating and we looked at the capsule. Only half the crystal was there.' It would have been impossible for him to have broken the capsule by ordinary means.

After Geller had paid a short visit to Professor Hasted's home, solid objects began to behave unpredictably:

A small ivory ornament appeared out of thin air, not flying, but dropping to the ground from about a foot [30 centimetres] above the floor. There was also the key of a French Empire clock that teleported from one room to the next. I found it on the floor, by the kitchen door, and put it back in its proper place. . . . I walked back into the kitchen and found it lying in the same place on the floor.

Uri Geller seems to have a psychokinetic ability (power of mind over matter) that he can only partially control or predict. Ironically, it is this very lack of control that, many people consider, argues for his genuineness – anything too glib implies rehearsal or sleight of hand.

This suspicion attached itself to the feats of many famous Victorian mediums. So many of them were proved to fake their seances that any curious phenomena attached to their movement became suspect. Even the founder of Theosophy, the controversial Madame Blavatsky, was frequently suspected of sleight of hand – for example, a whole teaset conveniently fell out of the sky during a picnic and, more tellingly, her 'teleported' messages allegedly from her Master in Tibet contained whole passages from a recently published American sermon – a fact that, while it does not directly challenge the reality

Above: Uri Geller, the Israeli sensitive, whose presence causes objects to apport

Below: 'a moonlight transit of Venus' – a contemporary impression of the teleportation across London of the large Mrs Guppy in 1871

of the teleported letter, reveals the Tibetan Master as a plagiarist and on the whole not the sort of guru whose word should be taken as gospel.

Another medium whose phenomena were both spectacular and open to question was Mrs Guppy who, while still Miss Nichol, produced apports of six variegated anemones, 15 chrysanthemums and assorted other flowers at a London seance in 1867.

One of her more startling feats, however, seems to be genuine. On the evening of June 3rd 1871 Mrs Guppy, attired in her night-gown (some reports say her underwear), was sitting quietly in the breakfast room of her Highbury home, busy with the household accounts. A friend was with her, when suddenly she disappeared and appeared in a room in Lamb's Conduit Street (a few miles away) where a seance was in progress, still clutching her accounts book and in a trance. That she was as solid in Lamb's Conduit Street as in Highbury was borne out by the fact that her materialisation caused some buffeting round the seance table. There was a heavy thud on the table and one of the sitters cried out 'Good God – there is something on my head!' One sympathises; Mrs Guppy was described as 'the biggest woman in London'. She weighed over 230 lbs (100 kilograms) and, as she was something of a figure of fun, the whole story, instead of being the psychic proof of the phenomenon of teleportation so many mediums were looking for, became the biggest joke for years.

Fort, with his theory of the cosmic joke, might have pointed out that Mrs Guppy's name, size and joke reputation were precisely why it was she and not, say, Queen Victoria, who was 'selected' for this astonishing psychical demonstration . . . and why it was a stage illusionist who dematerialised 'before your very eyes'.

The famous case of the 'Mary Celeste'

On 5 December 1872 the captain of the brigantine *Dei Gratia* sighted a ship sailing so clumsily that he went to investigate. The mystery deepened as he explored the abandoned *Mary Celeste*. Although showing signs of some storm damage, she was still sea-worthy. One lifeboat had apparently been launched (rather than having been washed overboard), but there was still plenty of fresh water aboard, provisions for six months were intact and the crew's clothes – including their oilskins – were hanging

on their pegs. On one bunk a child's toys lay as if left in mid-game. Everywhere there were signs of abrupt abandonment – however, the ship's navigation instruments and some papers were missing (although the log remained). The only signs of something bizarre were two long grooves apparently etched into the wood above the waterline, blood-like stains on the deck and on the captain's sword in his deserted cabin, and a mysterious cut in the ship's rail. What really happened? Did the crew fall victim to illness, insanity, homicide, suicide or the delusion that they were sinking? Were they abducted by giant sea-creatures or space-men, as some suggest? The theories are many, but it seems very likely that we shall never know for certain.

Who are the abductors?

What is the truth behind the phenomenon of mysterious disappearances? Who, or what, are the abductors? This chapter attempts to answer these questions and chronicles more cases of inexplicably vanishing people

PEOPLE HAVE BEEN DISAPPEARING mysteriously since the beginning of time, but the agencies blamed for abducting them have changed according to the spiritual preoccupations of the day. Gods, demons, fairies, spirits, and now UFOs show an astonishing predilection for what seems to be the random picking up and setting down – or picking up and not returning – of perfectly ordinary people.

In 1678 a Dr Moore and his three friends were touring Ireland. They put up for the night at an inn at Dromgreagh in Wicklow. Something prompted the doctor to tell his tale about how he had been abducted many times as a child by fairies, only to be rescued by the intervention of the local witch's magic. And even as he spoke the whole process went into motion again . . .

He saw a 'troop of men' come into the inn and drag him off with them. Frightening enough for him – but terrifying for the three witnesses, for all they saw was Dr Moore being pulled out of his chair and out of the room by an invisible but irresistible force. His friends made a grab at him but the force was too strong, and he vanished into the

Below: fairies abducting a human child, from a 19th-century book illustration. Folklore is full of tales of children being stolen by fairies, who leave their own fairy children – changelings – in their place

night. The innkeeper recommended they send for the local wise woman. She explained that the doctor had been abducted by the local fairies and was their prisoner in a nearby wood. She could break their hold on him, but her spell would only work for his release if he could be made to abstain from food and drink during his imprisonment. If not, he would return but would soon weaken and die. She cast her spell and they all waited.

Next morning at dawn Dr Moore came back to the inn, starving and thirsty, complaining that all the refreshments he had been offered during the night had inexplicably been dashed out of his hand. Unknown to him, the old woman's spell had been working and had finally secured his release – as morning came he had discovered he was suddenly alone near the inn.

The three witnesses attested to the story. It was published as a pamphlet and signed by one J. Cotham; a copy is now preserved in the British Museum.

Two thousand miles and nearly 300 years away, another story of abduction with witnesses reflects an entirely different preoccupation. On 5 November 1975 Travis Walton, a young forester, and his five workmates were driving to work near Snowflake, Arizona. They suddenly saw a bright light hovering over their truck. As the driver, Mike Rogers, stopped the car, Travis felt an extraordinary

compulsion to approach the light. He jumped out and rushed towards it. There was a sudden flash of light, and Travis hit the ground. Terrified, the others drove off. When they had calmed down, they returned to the same spot and instigated a thorough search that was to last for five days and cover miles of the Arizona desert and forest. Suspicion naturally fell on the five friends, but their distress seemed completely genuine and their story held up even under close questioning with the aid of a lie-detector.

Five days later, a confused and shaky Walton appeared in Heber, a small town close to Snowflake. His story tallied with that of his friends – as far as theirs went – but he added some amazing details. The beam of light had knocked him unconscious and then somehow drawn him up into a spacecraft in which he was examined by foetus-like creatures before being 'dumped' in Heber.

The 1880s saw a large number of disappearances from East London, known to this day as the 'West Ham disappearances'. One of the first victims was little Eliza Carter, who vanished from her home but later appeared in the street and spoke to some of her school friends. They tried to persuade her to

Above: Travis Walton, a young forestry worker who says he was mysteriously abducted by a UFO while driving to work near Snowflake, Arizona, USA on 5 November 1975. Five days later he reappeared, telling an amazing story of his 'flight' in the unknown craft

country station some mile and a half from my Sussex home. The train from London had arrived late, the bus had gone and no taxis were available. The rain was heavy and incessant. The time was 5.55 p.m. and I was expecting an important trunk call from overseas at 6 p.m. at home. The situation seemed desperate. To make matters worse, the station call box was out of order and some trouble on the line made access to the railway telephone impossible. In despair I sat down in the waiting room and having nothing better to do, I compared my watch with the station clock. Allowing for the fact that this is always kept two minutes in advance, I was able to confirm the fact that the exact time was 5.57 p.m. Three minutes to zero hour! What happened next I cannot say. When I came to myself I was standing in my hall at home, a good 20 minutes walk away, and the clock was striking six. My telephone call duly came through a few minutes later. Having finished my call, I awoke to the realisation that something very strange had happened. Then

go home to her family, but she said she couldn't – 'they' wouldn't let her. She was seen around West Ham for a couple of days before finally disappearing forever.

A similar case was that of Private Jerry Unwin of the US Army, who disappeared, reappeared, absented himself and appeared once more, before vanishing again on 1 August 1959.

The experience was not pleasant, and a far cry from the semi-mystical experience of the abductees portrayed in the film *Close encounters of the third kind*, but it was kin to the whole history of mysterious abductions.

The late psychic and writer Wellesley Tudor Pole recounted a strange tale of teleportation, in his book *The silent road* (1962):

On a wet and stormy night in December, 1952, I found myself at a

Above left: Eliza Carter, the 12-year-old schoolgirl who disappeared mysteriously in East London in January 1882. Her case was the first of a series of abductions that came to be known as the 'West Ham disappearances'

Above: a series of sketches showing the fate of one Amelia Jeffs, thought to be another victim of the West Ham disappearances. This time, however, there was no mystery: clues quickly led police to the discovery of the little girl's body

much to my surprise, I found that my shoes were dry and free from mud, and that my clothes showed no sign of damp or damage.

Like all such stories, there is something exasperatingly incomplete about this strange tale. Wellesley Tudor Pole has told all he can remember, but inevitably the phenomenon raises questions he cannot answer. As there were no witnesses in this case, no one will ever know how – or if – the teleportee disappeared. Did he literally vanish? Was he transported invisibly? How did he reappear? But at least one thing seems certain – what triggered off the teleporting agency seems to have been no less than the writer's own will. He was desperate to get home in time for his telephone call and his anxiety seems to have put into motion whatever natural law it is that governs the occurrence of the phenomenon.

Desire could also explain the bilocation of Sister Mary of Agreda (see page 33); intense piety and missionary zeal could have generated the unknown energies needed to transport a facsimile of herself to Mexico.

But in the annals of disappearing people there is no more controversial tale nor one stranger than the alleged 'Philadelphia experiment'. In 1943 there reportedly took place a horrifying experiment into invisibility involving a ship and its crew. This was not a psychic test, but a top-secret experiment of the United States Navy. According to Charles Berlitz and William Moore in their book *The Philadelphia experiment* (1979), the surviving witnesses to the experiment still suffer harrassment and have been repeatedly warned against discussing it by government agents.

A force field was created around the experimental ship – a destroyer – as it lay in a special berth in the Philadelphia Navy Yard. The crew could see one another normally but witnesses could only see the vague outline of both ship and men through the force field. They shimmered like a heat haze before

re-assuming normal shape and density. The effect on the crewmen involved was said to be appalling. The after-effects took various horrible forms: some of the men are said to have suffered a particularly harrowing form of spontaneous human combustion (described in an earlier volume) – bursting into flames that burned brightly for 18 days; others went mad, and yet others periodically became semi-transparent or partly invisible. Some died as a direct result of their experience.

An eyewitness claimed to have seen the entire experiment take place, and even to have thrust his arm into the force field that surged

> in a counterclockwise direction around the little experimental Navy ship . . . I watched the air all around the ship . . . turn slightly darker than all the other

One of the most extraordinary disappearances ever allegedly took place in 1943, when the US Navy is reported to have carried out a horrifying experiment in invisibility, and succeeded in making a destroyer, the USS *Eldridge* (bottom), together with its crew, disappear for a few minutes from its berth in the Philadelphia Navy Yard (below). However, as most of the evidence comes from a single witness, it is impossible to judge whether the experiment took place

> air . . . I saw, after a few minutes, a foggy green mist arise like a thin cloud. I think this must have been a mist of atomic particles. I watched as [it] became rapidly invisible to human eyes. And yet the precise shape of the keel and underhull of that ship remained impressed into the ocean water . . . The field had a sheet of pure electricity around it as it flowed . . . my entire body was not within that force field when it reached maximum strength density . . . and so I was not knocked down but my arm and hand was [sic] only pushed backward

The US Navy deny that the experiment took place. Yet the story is too persistent and has too much inner consistency to be dismissed entirely. If 'project invisibility' did take place, then it made scientific history – but compared to 'natural' disappearances it was clumsy and very dangerous.

The US Navy do have an interest in invisibility that can be verified, however. In September 1980 they made it known that they were experimenting with *radar* invisibility, but escaping a radar scan is a far cry from disappearing from human sight.

If it were possible to harness the 'natural force' that occasionally drags people from one place or plane of existence to another in a matter of seconds, or makes them invisible, then life as we know it would change completely. Whole armies could suddenly materialise unexpectedly in the country of their foes; spies could invisibly slip past the guards at top secret installations; criminals dematerialise when the law draws too close. . . .

Yet perhaps the clue, such as it is , lies in the very randomness of the phenomenon. Perhaps there is no natural force but, paradoxically, a random law creating freak effects for their own sake. This suggests a governing intelligence, a cosmic joker like the one who perhaps stage-manages the manifestations of the Loch Ness Monster, UFOs, bigfoot . . . and who jams the witnesses' cameras at the critical moments or contrives to discredit witnesses. So we come full circle – is the joker a god, a demon, a fairy, a spirit or a UFO?

Researcher Ivan T. Sanderson said of the UFO phenomenon, 'It cannot be all bunkum yet some of its implications are so bizarre as to be almost beyond comprehension.' This could well apply to all 'Fortean' phenomena. Those who disappear for ever – do they go to some other world, some other plane, or do they find themselves in that other unexplored region, the furthest reaches of the human mind? If abductions are ascribed to the agencies currently in vogue – put, as Fort said, 'in terms of the familiar' – then the phenomenon must be at least partly 'in the mind'. Yet the disappearances are real.

It is likely that such phenomena will remain unexplained until a comprehensive explanation for all strange phenomena can be formulated. Until then – who knows?

Apparitions, many researchers believe, exist only in the human mind. But what of the art, allegedly practised by Tibetan adepts, of making thought forms materialise so strongly that they can be seen by other people? FRANCIS KING investigates

CONDITIONS ON THE ROAD from China to Lhasa, the forbidden capital city of Tibet, were even worse than usual in the winter of 1923 to 1924. Nevertheless, small numbers of travellers, mostly pilgrims wishing to obtain spiritual merit by visiting the holy city and seeing its semi-divine ruler, the Dalai Lama, struggled onwards through the bitter winds and heavy snow. Among them was an elderly woman who appeared to be a peasant from some distant province of the god-king's empire.

The woman was poorly dressed and equipped. Her red woollen skirt and waistcoat, her quilted jacket, and her cap with its lambskin earflaps, were worn and full of holes. From her shoulder hung an ancient leather bag, black with dirt. In this were the provisions for her journey: barley meal, a piece of dried bacon, a brick of compressed tea, a tube of rancid butter, and a little salt and soda.

With her black hair coated with grease and her dark brown face, she looked like a typical peasant woman. But her hair was really white, dyed with Chinese ink, and her complexion took its colour from oil mixed with cocoa and crushed charcoal. For this Tibetan peasant woman was in reality Alexandra David-Neel, a Frenchwoman who, 30 years before, had been an opera singer of note who had been warmly congratulated by Jules Massenet for her performance in the title role of his opera *Manon*. In the intervening years

Mme David-Neel had travelled to strange places and had undergone even stranger experiences. These had included meeting a magician with the ability to cast spells to hurl flying rice cakes at his enemies, and learning the techniques of *tumo*, an occult art that enables its adepts to sit naked amid the Himalayan snows. Most extraordinary of all, she had constructed, by means of mental and psychic exercises, a *tulpa* – a phantom form born solely from the imagination, and yet so strongly vitalised by the adept's visualisation and will that it actually becomes visible to other people. A tulpa is, to put it another way, an extremely powerful example of what occultists term a thought form.

To understand the nature of the tulpa one has to appreciate that, as far as Tibetan Buddhists (and most Western occultists) are concerned, thought is far more than an intellectual function. Every thought, they believe, affects the 'mind-stuff' that permeates the world of matter in very much the same way as a stone thrown into a lake makes ripples upon the water's surface. A thought, in other words, produces a 'thought ripple'.

Usually these thought ripples have only a short life. They decay almost as soon as they are created and make no lasting impression on the mind-stuff interpenetrating the physical plane. If, however, the thought is particularly intense, the product of deep passion or fear, or if it is of long duration, the subject of much brooding and meditation, the thought ripple builds the mind-stuff into a more permanent thought form, one that has a longer and more intense life.

Tulpas and other thought forms are not considered by Tibetan Buddhists to be 'real' – but neither, according to them, is the world of matter that seemingly surrounds us. Both are illusory. As a Buddhist classic from the first century AD expresses it:

All phenomena are originally in the

Below: pilgrims approach the holy city of Lhasa, the forbidden capital of Tibet, in a photograph taken in the 1930s; this modern photograph (below right) testifies to the continuing practice of this arduous form of religious devotion. One of the most remarkable pilgrims to have undertaken this journey was Alexandra David-Neel (right, with a companion, the lama Yongden) who, in the 1920s, travelled throughout Tibet and learned many of the secrets of the Tibetan Buddhists – including the art of making thought forms materialise

The word made flesh

mind and have really no outward form; therefore, as there is no form, it is an error to think that anything is there. All phenomena merely arise from false notions in the mind. If the mind is independent of these false ideas, then all phenomena disappear.

If the beliefs about thought forms held by Tibetan Buddhists, by mystics and magicians, are justified, then many ghostly happenings, hauntings, and cases of localities endowed with a strong 'psychic atmosphere' are easily explained. It seems plausible, for example, that the thought forms created by the violent and passionate mental processes of a murderer, supplemented by the terror stricken emotions of a victim, could linger around the scene of the crime for months, years, or even centuries. This could produce intense depression and anxiety in those who visited the 'haunted' spot and, if the thought

forms were sufficiently vivified and powerful, 'apparitions', such as a re-enactment of the crime, might be witnessed by people possessed of psychic sensitivity.

Sometimes, it is claimed by students of the occult, the 'spirits' that haunt a particular spot are tulpas, thought forms that have been deliberately created by a sorcerer for his own purposes.

The existence of extremely potent thought forms that re-enact the past would explain the worldwide reports of visitors to old battlefields 'witnessing' military encounters that took place long before. The sites of the battle of Naseby, which took place during England's 17th century Civil War, and of the 1942 commando raid on Dieppe during World War Two are among battlefields that enjoy such ghostly reputations.

A tulpa is no more than an extremely powerful thought form, no different in its essential nature from many other ghostly apparitions. Where, however, it does differ from a normal thought form is that it has come into existence, not as a result of an accident, a side effect of a mental process, but as the result of a deliberate act of will.

The word tulpa is a Tibetan one, but there are adepts in almost every part of the world who believe they are able to manufacture these beings by first drawing together and coagulating some of the mind-stuff of the Universe into a form, and then transferring to it some of their own vitality.

In Bengal, home of much Indian occultism, the technique is called *kriya shakti* ('creative power'), and is studied and practised by the adepts of Tantrism, a religio-magical system concerned with the spiritual aspects of sexuality numbering both Hindus and Buddhists among its devotees. Initiates of 'left-handed' Tantric cults – that is to say, cults in which men and women engage in ritual sexual intercourse for mystical and magical purposes – are considered particularly skilled in *kriya shakti*. This is because it is thought that the intense physical and cerebral excitement of the orgasm engenders quite exceptionally vigorous thought forms.

Many Tibetan mystical techniques originated in Bengal, particularly in Bengali Tantrism, and there is a very strong resemblance between the physical, mental and spiritual exercises used by the Tantric yogis of Bengal and the secret inner disciplines of Tibetan Buddhism. It thus seems likely that Tibetans originally derived their theories about tulpas, and their methods of creating these strange beings, from Bengali practitioners of *kriya shakti*.

Students of tulpa magic begin their training in the art of creating these thought beings by adopting one of the many gods or goddesses of the Tibetan pantheon as a 'tutelary deity' – a sort of patron saint. It must be emphasised that, while Tibetan initiates regard the gods respectfully, they do not look upon them with any great admiration. For, according to Buddhist belief, although the gods have great powers and are, in a sense, 'supernatural', they are just as much slaves of illusion, just as much trapped in the wheel of birth, death, and rebirth, as the humblest peasant.

The student retires to a hermitage or other secluded place and meditates on his tutelary deity, known as a *yidam*, for many hours. He combines a contemplation of the spiritual attributes traditionally associated with the *yidam* with visualisation exercises designed to build up in the mind's eye an image of the *yidam* as it is portrayed in paintings and statues.

To keep his concentration upon the *yidam*, to ensure that in every waking moment there is a single-pointed devotion to that being, the student continually chants traditional mystic phrases associated with the deity he serves.

He also constructs the *kyilkhors* – literally circles, but actually symbolic diagrams that may be of any shape – believed sacred to his god. Sometimes he will draw these with coloured inks on paper or wood, sometimes he will engrave them on copper or silver, sometimes he will outline them on his floor with coloured powders.

The preparation of the *kyilkhors* must be undertaken with care, for the slightest deviation from the traditional pattern associated with a particular *yidam* is believed to be extremely dangerous, putting the unwary student in peril of obsession, madness, death, or a stay of thousands of years in one of the 'hells' of Tibetan cosmology.

It is interesting to compare this belief with the idea, strongly held by many Western occultists, that if a magician engaged in 'evoking a spirit to visible appearance' draws his protective magical circle incorrectly, he will be 'torn in pieces'.

Below: a Buddhist monk with drum and incense stick. The rigorous mental and physical discipline taught by Buddhism enables some of its followers to attain paranormal powers; in her book *Initiations and initiates in Tibet* Alexandra David-Neel tells of a man (right, standing on left) who was reputed to be able to hypnotise and cause death at a distance

Wolf at the door

In her book *Psychic self defence* (1930), the occultist Dion Fortune (left) relates how she once 'formulated a were-wolf accidentally'.

She had this alarming experience while she was brooding about her feelings of resentment against someone who had hurt her. Lying on her bed, she was thinking of the terrifying wolf-monster of Norse mythology, Fenrir, when suddenly she felt a large grey wolf materialise beside her. She was aware of its body pressing against hers.

From her reading about thought forms, she knew she must gain control of the beast immediately. So she dug her

Eventually, if the student has persisted with the prescribed exercises, he 'sees' his *yidam*, at first nebulously and briefly, but then persistently and with complete – and sometimes terrifying – clarity.

But this is only the first stage of the process. Meditation, visualisation of the *yidam*, the repetition of spells and contemplation of mystic diagrams is continued until the tulpa in the form of the *yidam* actually materialises. The devotee can feel the touch of the tulpa's feet when he lays his head upon them, he can see the creature's eye following him as he moves about, he can even conduct conversations with it.

Thoughts made visible

Eventually the tulpa may be prepared to leave the vicinity of the *kyilkhors* and accompany the devotee on journeys. If the tulpa has been fully vitalised it will by now often be visible to others besides its creator.

Alexandra David-Neel tells how she 'saw' a phantom of this sort which, curiously enough, had not yet become visible to its creator. At the time Mme David-Neel had developed a great interest in Buddhist art. One afternoon she was visited by a Tibetan painter who specialised in portraying the 'wrathful deities'; as he approached she was astonished to see behind him the misty form of one of these much feared and rather unpleasant beings. She approached the phantom and stretched out an arm towards it; she felt as if she were 'touching a soft object whose substance gave way under the slight push'.

The painter told her that he had for some weeks been engaged in magical rites calling on the god whose form she had seen, and that he had spent the entire morning painting its picture.

Intrigued by this experience, Mme David-Neel set about making a tulpa for herself. To avoid being influenced by the many Tibetan paintings and images she had seen on her travels, she decided to 'make', not a god or goddess, but a fat, jolly-looking monk whom she could visualise very clearly.

Two Tibetans dressed as gods. Tibetan Buddhists regard their gods with reverence, but believe that they are no less trapped in the cycles of birth, death and rebirth than any human being – and even attempt to make the gods materialise by a sustained effort of concentration

elbow into its hairy ribs and exclaimed, 'If you can't behave yourself, you will have to go on the floor,' and pushed it off the bed. The animal disappeared through the wall.

The story was not yet over, however, for another member of the household said she had seen the eyes of the wolf in the corner of her room. Dion Fortune realised she must destroy the creature. Summoning the beast, she saw a thin thread joining it to her. She began to imagine she was drawing the life out of the beast along this thread. The wolf faded to a formless grey mass – and ceased to exist.

She began to concentrate her mind.

She retired to a hermitage and for some months devoted every waking minute to exercises in concentration and visualisation. She began to get brief glimpses of the monk out of the corner of her eye. He became more solid and lifelike in appearance – and eventually, when she left her hermitage and started on a caravan journey, he included himself in the party, becoming clearly visible and performing actions that she had neither commanded nor consciously expected him to do. He would, for instance, walk and stop to look around him as a traveller might do; sometimes Mme David-Neel even felt his robe brush against her, and once a hand seemed to touch her shoulder.

Mme David-Neel's tulpa eventually began to develop in an unexpected and unwished for manner.

He grew leaner, his expression became malignant, he was 'troublesome and bold'. One day a herdsman who brought Mme David-Neel a present of some butter saw the tulpa in her tent – and mistook it for a real monk. It had got out of control. Her creation turned into what she called a 'day-nightmare' and she decided to get rid of it. It took her six months of concentrated effort and meditation to do so.

If this, and many similar stories told in Tibet, are to be believed, the creation of a tulpa is not a matter to be undertaken lightly. It is a fascinating example of the power of the human mind to create its own reality.

When impossible demands are made of us we say 'we can't be in two places at once' – but in 1845 a French teacher, Emilie Sagée, apparently was. Her well-witnessed bilocation was specially researched by COLIN GODMAN, who tells the story

IN 1853 THE AMERICAN WRITER Robert Dale Owen paused while in London to hear a story told by a young German woman that was to become a classic of its kind. It was the apparently well-documented story of a *doppelgänger*, the exact double that is supposed, according to legend, to stalk us all, but that stays just out of sight. The 'double' in this story – or 'fetch' as the Victorians chose to name it – stayed out of sight of its victim but nevertheless it evoked widespread terror. This 'fetch' was that of a French schoolmistress. And it was seen not only by the young woman telling the story, but by over 40 of her companions at school. Dale Owen made a note of every detail of the story, and it was soon to find a place in the annals of late 19th-century psychical research.

Julie von Güldenstubbe, the second daughter of the Baron von Güldenstubbe, was 13 in 1845 and attended a school for

Above: Robert Dale Owen (1801–1877), the American writer who helped to popularise the strange tale of Emilie Sagée

Below: a scene from the BBC's Sagée story. Emilie, played by Juliet Harmer, was seen in the school garden while her double supervised the girls in the classroom

daughters of the nobility. This exclusive school, the Pensionat von Neuwelcke, was said to be 36 miles (58 kilometres) from the port of Riga and 3½ miles (6 kilometres) from Wolmar in Livonia (now part of the USSR). Lessons were conducted in German, the language of the landowners and ruling classes. The principal, Herr Buch, a distinguished Moravian scholar, had appointed a French teacher, Mademoiselle Emilie Sagée, to the staff in 1845, and it was with her that Baroness Julie's story was concerned.

The French teacher said that she was born in Dijon 32 years before she took up her post at Neuwelcke. She was fair skinned, with chestnut hair and blue eyes, and was fairly tall and slim. The pupils described her as having a sweet and lovable nature. The superintendents at the school were entirely satisfied with her work and were impressed by her gaiety, intelligence and education.

Everything promised well for Mlle Sagée's career at Neuwelcke – but within a few weeks of her arrival she became the focus of rumour and gossip in the school. It seemed that Emilie could be – literally – in two places at once. If she was reported to be in a particular part of the school someone would contradict, saying, 'Oh no, she cannot be there; I just passed her on the stairs' or in some distant corridor. Individual pupils

Me and my shadow

repeated this sort of confusion time and time again, but the teachers dismissed the girls' stories as silly mistakes.

But naturally the most excitement was caused by the rumours that followed the first appearance of the 'double' to a number of witnesses. Mlle Sagée was giving a lesson to Julie von Güldenstubbe and 12 other girls. The subject of the lesson varied slightly with

Soon after Emilie Sagée arrived at the small *pensionat* (boarding school) in 1845 the girls started spreading rumours that their new French teacher had been seen in two places at the same time. Naturally all eyes were on Mlle Sagée and the strain on her must have been extraordinary. She is said to have had moral support from Julie von Güldenstubbe (left, played by Lesley Manville)

Below: the real Emilie takes a lesson – but is soon to be joined by her double, or 'fetch', which mirrored her every move; however, only the real Emilie held chalk

each storyteller: for example, one suggested Emilie was energetically demonstrating a mathematical theorem on the blackboard; Julie said the lesson was French grammar. What *was* agreed on was that Emilie Sagée was standing at the blackboard with her back to the class. Suddenly, a second 'Emilie' materialised at Mlle Sagée's side. The two were exactly alike and went through the same movements, synchronising perfectly. The only difference was that the real Emilie had chalk in her hand but the fetch had none; it merely mimed the teacher's action as she wrote on the board. This story caused a great sensation at Neuwelcke, particularly as all 13 pupils in the class agreed precisely in their description of what they had seen.

A spirited imitation

In the following weeks the fetch was seen on a number of occasions. For instance it appeared at dinner, standing behind Mlle Sagée and imitating her movements as she ate. But, as in the classroom, the double's hands were empty. On these occasions the schoolgirls were not alone in seeing Emilie's fetch; the servants also reportedly saw the figure behind the chair.

One of Julie's schoolfriends was badly frightened by the fetch. Fräulein Antonie von Wrangel was in a group invited to a local rural festivity and she was getting ready in her room. Emilie was helping her to fasten her dress. There was a mirror hanging behind them and Antonie turned to catch sight of two identical mademoiselles, each

doing up her dress. Startled, she fainted clean away.

However, the fetch did not always mirror Emilie Sagée's actions. Sometimes, Baroness Julie reported, it would behave quite independently. For example, the real Mlle Sagée would rise from her chair – but her double would remain seated. Antonie von Wrangel and a group of friends looked after Emilie when she was taken ill with a feverish cold. The girls took turns to read to her as she recovered in bed. Antonie was alone with her when she noticed the colour suddenly drain from Mlle Sagée's face. She was so pale she seemed about to faint, and Antonie asked if she was feeling worse. Emilie answered in a weak and trembling voice that she was not, but her frightened look alarmed Antonie. A few moments later Antonie looked up from her book to see the fetch walking up and down the room, apparently in excellent health. This time Fräulein von Wrangel remained calm and did not tell Emilie what she had seen. When she came downstairs from Mlle Sagée's room she told the others exactly what she had experienced. On that occasion there had been only one witness – but the next and most remarkable appearance of the fetch was witnessed by the whole school.

This time all 42 pupils were gathered in

Left: pupil Antonie von Wrangel (actress Lalla Ward) faints after seeing Mlle Sagée's 'fetch' in the mirror while the teacher was helping her dress. Fräulein von Wrangel had happened to glance in a mirror that was hanging behind her – and saw two Emilie Sagées, one fastening her dress, the other, perfectly synchronised, going through the motions of doing so

the school hall to do their sewing and embroidery. Four french windows opened onto a corridor leading to the large garden in front of the house. The weather was fine and the girls had a clear view of the garden, where Mlle Sagée could be clearly seen picking flowers.

The girls sat round a long table and the teacher sat at one end, supervising their work. After a little while she got up to leave them alone for some reason. Her chair did not remain empty for long however, as suddenly Mlle Sagée appeared in it. The girls turned their eyes to the garden and, sure enough, there was Emilie. Although still gathering flowers, her movements were slow and languid as though – as the girls later remarked – she had suddenly been overcome with fatigue and tiredness. All the while her fetch sat silent and motionless.

Although afraid, the girls were getting used to the strange phenomena and two of the boldest among them decided to take a closer look at the fetch. They approached the chair, determined to touch the apparition. Stretching out their hands they encountered a slight resistance in the air surrounding it, such as a thin film of muslin or crêpe-de-chine might offer.

One brave girl tried to pass between the chair and the table – and stepped right through the figure in the chair. Emilie's double did not react, however, remaining seated until, a short time later, it slowly disappeared. As before, the girls turned to the garden to watch the real Mlle Sagée again gathering flowers with her usual animation.

All 42 girls agreed on what they had witnessed and some questioned their teacher

Below: rural Latvia, the Eastern European setting for the Sagée saga

soon after. They asked how she had felt in the garden and if she had experienced anything special. Emilie answered that she had noticed the other teacher leaving the girls unattended. Emilie had had a clear view of the empty chair and recalled wishing the teacher had not left her pupils alone to waste their time and probably get up to mischief. She had wished, she added, that she could have been sitting there to keep an eye on the girls so they would get on with their work.

Over a year had passed since Emilie Sagée had arrived at Neuwelcke and the girls had

Mixed doubles

To come face to face with one's *doppelgänger*, or double, is a rare but chilling experience. The German poet Goethe (1749–1832) once met 'himself' coming towards him up a garden path; according to European folklore this should have been a sign of his imminent death, but Goethe lived for some years after his experience.

The doppelgänger, or in Victorian terms the 'fetch', is always said to be indistinguishable from the real person and is apparently solid-looking. However, much more common in the archives of psychical research is the ghostly double, or 'wraith', sometimes called the *ka* by occultists. This is believed to be attached to the physical body by an invisible cord that can stretch (left) to accommodate astral travel during sleep and that snaps at death.

Emilie Sagée's double seems to have harmed only her career, but it is said that the wraith, when disengaged from the body, can leave it prey to possession by all manner of evil spirits.

had plenty of opportunities to see and talk about the fetch – or doppelgänger as they must have called it. They noticed that there was an apparently vampiristic relationship or link between Emilie and her double. When the fetch appeared strong and clear Emilie seemed to suffer as a consequence, as though the wraith drew its power from the living woman. When she was busy and absorbed in a task she would suddenly be overcome with weakness and tiredness; at just such moments the double would be seen.

Emilie herself seems not to have seen her

Below: a music lesson is interrupted by a fresh rumour about the 'two Mlle Sagées'. In a closed community of impressionable adolescents the stories of the teacher's 'fetch' spread like wildfire until they became a craze. Discipline became difficult to maintain; in short, excellent teacher though she was, Mlle Sagée had to leave the school

fetch while at Neuwelcke but she would be instantly alerted to its presence by the reactions of the girls around her. She also came to realise that the return of her strength and energy signalled the moment that the double disappeared.

How did the school react to the events of 1845 and 1846? All the pupils, to some degree, had witnessed the phenomena; so Emilie, unwittingly, caused considerable commotion at Neuwelcke. Although she was very popular among the girls, the more timid gradually became disturbed by her presence. They told their parents, and the school directors noted with growing concern that fewer and fewer girls returned to the Pensionat at the beginning of each term.

The reasons they gave for leaving the school varied, but Herr Buch and his colleagues were left in little doubt as to the true reason for Neuwelcke's fall from favour. Buch must have been gravely tempted to dismiss Mlle Sagée, but she was, after all, a perfectly good teacher. She seemed, he realised, to be the innocent victim of something quite beyond her control. It would create a scandal to dismiss such an excellent teacher on what must have seemed like grounds of insanity – and scandals at Neuwelcke were to be avoided at all costs.

However, Julie von Güldenstubbe tells us that the school's hopes for normality were in vain. Eighteen months after Emilie Sagée had taken up her post at Neuwelcke the school rollcall of 42 had dwindled to a mere 12. Something had to be done.

Emilie Sagée was not the only 19th-century girl to have a well-witnessed double, as the archives of psychical research show. But, ask COLIN GODMAN and LINDSAY ST CLAIRE, was the evidence for these bizarre events just too good to be true? What really happened?

Seeing double

EIGHTEEN MONTHS after the young French teacher Emilie Sagée came to the Pensionat at Neuwelcke, in Livonia (now in the USSR), the number of pupils had dwindled from 42 in 1845 to a mere dozen. Emilie's doppelgänger, or double, was blamed for this change in fortune, and at the risk of scandal the school's directors had no choice but to dismiss Mlle Sagée.

Although her professional qualifications and conduct were beyond reproach, Emilie had to leave. As long as she remained at Neuwelcke, she was told, the school's future was at risk. Emilie's dismay is easy to imagine, and Julie von Güldenstubbe – whose

account forms the basis of this story – recalled Emilie exclaiming, 'Alas, this is the nineteenth time: What am I to do?'

To have been dismissed from 19 teaching posts in such a short career may seem rather improbable, but Emilie explained to her young friends that she had begun teaching in 1829, when she was barely 16. She had been dismissed each time for more or less the same reason: two 'Emilie Sagées' were one too many for every school. It would have come as little comfort to Emilie to note that things improved at Neuwelcke after she left. And within a term or two the nobility resumed sending their daughters to the Pensionat. Peace had returned to the school.

Julie did not immediately lose contact with Mlle Sagée. Although she did not see her for a while after the dismissal, she learned

Top: two of the schoolgirls at the Pensionat von Neuwelcke who were witnesses to Emilie Sagée's 'fetch', from the dramatised story made by the BBC in the 1970s for their *Leap in the dark* television series. Introduced by Colin Wilson (above), the series was well-researched – although hard facts about the Sagée case proved difficult to come by

that Emilie had gone to live with a sister-in-law who had several young children. The young Baroness went to visit her and found that the toddlers knew all about the French woman. They said they had two 'Aunt Emilies'.

Unfortunately, Emilie Sagée's recorded story ends there. Julie lost contact with her completely when her former teacher disappeared into the heartland of Russia some time in the 1850s.

What do we really know about Emilie Sagée? Apart from her unfortunate teaching record we know she claimed to be 32 years old when she arrived in Neuwelcke in 1845 and that she gave her place of birth as Dijon, France.

When the authors began researching this case in 1976 they hoped to find at least some record of an Emilie Sagée's birth in Dijon in 1813. Every available source in the town was searched, to no avail. The writer Camille Flammarion, however, had been more fortunate. In his book *Death and its mystery* (1922) he writes about Mlle Sagée and records his own search for her origins during 1895. He describes a fruitless hunt for civic records of a family named Sagée – but he did find a note of the birth of a child named 'Octavie Saget'; a 'natural' (illegitimate) child born on 3 January 1813.

Like Mlle Sagée, Octavie would, therefore, have been 32 in 1845. Flammarion ventured to suggest that Octavie and Emilie were one and the same; the change in name occasioned, perhaps, by the young teacher's shame about her illegitimacy.

Emilie's pupil, Julie von Güldenstubbe, was at Neuwelcke throughout Mlle Sagée's short stay, but she was only 13 and may well have misremembered the spelling of her teacher's name. Flammarion knew Julie and her brother, the Baron Güldenstubbe, in the 1860s. They were much the same age and he described them as totally sincere, a little mystical in inclination, but of the utmost integrity. Julie's brother had published a book in Paris in 1857 entitled *La realité des spirits et le phénomène de leur écriture directe* ('The reality of spirits and the phenomenon of their direct writing').

Camille Flammarion was born in 1842 and was a distinguished astronomer at the

Paris Observatory when he met Julie. Although a scientist, he was intrigued by the paranormal and by Julie's story.

The first account of the case was written by Robert Dale Owen. His background was very different from Flammarion's. Dale Owen was born in 1801 in Glasgow, the son of the famous social reformer, Robert Owen, who created experimental communities on both sides of the Atlantic. In old age Robert Owen's socialism gave way to Spiritualism and this had influenced Dale. After joining his father in Indiana, in the USA, Robert Dale Owen went into politics, entered Congress, supported Emancipation and became one of the chief advocates of Spiritualism in America. In 1859 he completed his book *Footfalls on the boundary of another world*; in it he included an account of his meeting with Julie, giving her version of the events surrounding Emilie Sagée.

The third source of material about Emilie Sagée is the Russian writer Alexander Aksakov. He came from an important literary family and became a distinguished physiologist at St Petersburg (now Leningrad) University. He was the same age as Julie and

Above: Dijon, France, where Mlle Sagée claimed to have been born in 1813. Yet research failed to reveal any record of her birth, although an 'Octavie Saget' – an illegitimate child – is noted in the register of births at about the right date. Could Octavie and Emilie have been one and the same?

Right: Riga, now part of Latvia. The Sagée story places the school 36 miles (58 kilometres) from here – but no 'Neuwelcke' could be found by the BBC research team

shared her interest in Spiritualism. He was to become the most important Russian parapsychologist of the last century and his book *Animismus und spiritismus*, published in Leipzig in 1890, contains the Emilie Sagée story.

As before, Julie von Güldenstubbe was credited as the source of the information, but Aksakov added a few insights of his own concerning Emilie's personality. He points out that although Emilie enjoyed good physical health, she had a nervous, excitable disposition. In itself this is not inconsistent with the schoolgirls' description of her as 'quiet and friendly', but it does suggest that she may have been under more strain than Julie and the other girls realised.

An elusive place

The school at Neuwelcke proves harder to track down than Emilie herself. All the accounts locate Neuwelcke 36 miles (58 kilometres) from Riga and $3\frac{1}{2}$ miles (6 kilometres) from Wolmar – but Wolmar, or Valmiera as it has been renamed, lies 75 miles (120 kilometres) from Riga. In itself the error may not be significant, but it does raise the question: did Neuwelcke ever exist? Unfortunately, the Latvian Legation have been unable to identify such a place. There is a farm (which has never been a school) near Valmiera called 'Jaunvelki' but that is the nearest that the Latvians can find to 'Neuwelcke' – not a very convincing link.

However, the loss of the Neuwelcke connection need not be too discouraging. Livonia itself has experienced many changes of identity over the years. The small country had long been hotly disputed by Poland, Sweden and Russia. In the 1800s Russia

ruled Livonia, but the country was still controlled by the rich German families who owned large estates there. The whole expanse of flat peatbogs, lakes and forests became the Republic of Latvia in 1918, bounded by Estonia, Lithuania, Russia and the Baltic Sea. Since 1940 Latvia has been part of the USSR.

How does the Emilie Sagée case fit into contemporary knowledge? It is possible to discount the traditional anecdotes of astral projection or out-of-the-body experiences. All such cases imply an effort of will to 'project' the subject or some sort of perception while 'out of the body'. In Emilie's case there is no evidence that she ever projected her 'fetch' of her own volition or that she recorded any sensations while 'in' her double.

For 100 years the Emilie Sagée case has attracted such labels as illusion, hallucination, mass hysteria and the like. But there is no evidence that the schoolgirls all suffered from any marked nervous disorder that may have encouraged them to hallucinate. 'Hallucinations' and 'illusions' are commonly understood to be the result of the brain misinterpreting unusual data fed into it by our senses. In other words what we see is merely a subjective interpretation of the information sent to our brain from our eyes, based largely on our personal experience – and expectation.

Optical illusions are often the result of trying to make sense of incomplete data; in fact, often a small sensory input is turned, by our ever-rational brains, into something different; it can become almost anything

Two by two

In the book *Phantasms of the living* (1886) by SPR founders Gurney, Myers and Podmore, there appear stories of other 'Emilies'.

Like Mlle Sagée, Lucy Eden could be in two places at once. In the autumn of 1845 a party of young people were staying at Cherington, a house near Shipston-on-Stour in Warwickshire, England (below). Although Lucy was 17 and her cousins much the same age, they were playing hide-and-seek. Lucy was clearly seen wearing a brown and white dress, standing under a tree in the orchard. Her cousins gave chase, and Lucy ran out into the cowyard, where, to the amazement of the others, she disappeared. But Lucy protested that she had been hiding in the wash-house with another cousin – who verified her story.

Lucy's 'fetch' appeared again in the spring of 1847 at her father's rectory at Leigh in Essex. Lucy had mumps, but she was up and about, although her face was bandaged. One morning the nursery maid, Caroline, passed Lucy walking from the drawing room to the library. Soon after, the Edens' maid asked Caroline where Lucy was. But the library was empty. Lucy was found in her bedroom where she had been, she claimed, all morning. Caroline refused to admit she had been mistaken, having particularly noted the bandages on Lucy's face.

Lucy, like Emilie Sagée, never saw her own fetch. But Sarah Jane Hall saw *her* double in 1863 in her home, Sibberton, near Wansford (now in Cambridgeshire). One night at supper Sarah's fetch was seen standing by the sideboard. Four people saw the figure: Sarah, her husband, and a cousin and her husband. They all saw Sarah's double distinctly, and her husband said: 'It is Sarah.' But the apparition, which had looked quite real, vanished. Had Mr Hall 'suggested' the identity of the apparition to the others? If not, what had they all seen?

– as long as it fits the pattern that suits our subconscious minds (a fact exploited by stage illusionists and the theatre in general). One can imagine an old house, ill-lit with flickering candles, where shadows and reflections create convincing illusions of sinister figures; a spurious reality created from insufficient information.

Before your very eyes

The brain demands logic; it needs to 'rationalise' the data with which it is presented. This appears to be an intelligent response to confusing sights – perhaps the only way of keeping sane in many circumstances. Optical illusions such as those produced by candlelight, sunshine streaming through trees in an orchard, or a flash of white that perhaps suggested a fetch's handkerchief, go some way towards explaining illusory fetches. But neither optical illusions nor mental rationalisations explain why 42 schoolgirls at Neuwelcke consistently agreed that there were two Mlle Sagées.

However, the 'risky shift' effect noted by modern psychologists may throw some light on the Sagée case. This is based on the observation that when individuals bring their beliefs to a group discussion they often leave with much more extreme attitudes than they started with. Psychologists maintain that this is an unconscious result of the group discussion or argument, and that these polarised opinions tend to be lasting. These 'risky shifts' can occur in any group; we can speculate that the school at Neuwelcke – isolated, enclosed and something of an aristocratic hothouse – would provide an ideal propagating medium for the phenomenon.

But does this theory throw any light on the Emilie Sagée story? The evidence in its

Is seeing believing? During a severe drought a mirage of water appears behind Thomson's gazelles on the parched Sambura plains of Kenya

A 19th-century allegorical painting by G.A. Roche-grosse, illustrating the effects of human credulity. A single rumour of a paranormal being seen in the sky ends in this tangled mass of hysterical humanity

favour is tempting: we discover that events began quietly, as single rumours that circulated swiftly, building into 'a ceaseless discussion', a kind of schoolgirl craze. After a time the events began to be viewed as something genuine – and very strange. And when the events grew even more bizarre, the number of convinced witnesses in the school also grew.

This is precisely what would be expected when a 'risky shift' occurs; there was no single, striking initial event, just the slow accumulation of gossip. But group discussions seemed, true to the 'risky shift' effect, to have dramatically reinforced their belief in Emilie's doppelgänger. That is why, ironically, the schoolgirls' 'perfect agreement' about what they witnessed is less convincing than if they had disagreed, even in trivial ways, about what they saw. Perfect unanimity among witnesses is virtually unknown. Even striking incidents produce widely varying descriptions – as any police force will testify. Total unanimity is the result of either pre-arranged agreement – a hoax or deliberate perjury – or more innocent, but intense, discussion and rationalisation.

That, then, is the psychologist's view of the little evidence we possess. The truth of what happened in Livonia in 1845 will never be known. Was Emilie Sagée's doppelgänger simply the product of gossip, reinforced by hysterical group discussion, and later recorded as fact by the mystically inclined Julie von Güldenstubbe?

There seems no doubt that the girls genuinely believed that Mlle Sagée was haunted by her fetch. At the Pensionat von Neuwelcke it seems that the old adage 'seeing is believing' was turned on its head: for a few bizarre months between 1845 and 1846 'believing', for 42 young girls, became even better than 'seeing'.

Gone but not forgotten

Stories abound of people disappearing in mysterious circumstances, never to be seen again. But, argues PAUL BEGG, these tales should be examined closely: many have simpler explanations – and some are pure fiction

SOME CURIOUS, inexplicable, and sometimes very frightening things have happened in this 'ordinary' world of ours, haven't they? Just look at all the books you can buy about ghosts, ESP, the Bermuda Triangle, ancient astronauts, mysterious disappearances, bigfoot, the Loch Ness monster. A whole host of things that are incredible yet indisputably true. Or are they?

It is a mistake to believe everything you read. Alas, that is a truism that can be applied less to newspapers than to books about the mysterious, the unexplained and the paranormal. Look at any display of books on these subjects and it is almost guaranteed that a great many of them will be about what Arthur C. Clarke has called 'Mysteries of the Zeroeth Kind – the mental junk food of our generation.' As he said in *Arthur C. Clarke's mysterious world* (1980):

> The only mystery about *these* is that anyone ever thought they were mysterious. The classic example is the Bermuda Triangle, though this has not prevented countless writers, some of whom may even believe the rubbish they are regurgitating, repeating the

In December 1900 three lighthouse keepers vanished from the Eilean Mor lighthouse (below) off the west coast of Scotland. James Ducat, Donald McArthur and Thomas Marshall were there when Joseph Moore left for shore leave on the 6th, but when he returned on the 26th they were gone. The beacon was not working and two sets of oilskins and boots were missing. The log told how a fierce storm had raged. On the 12th, Marshall had written in the log, 'Never seen such a storm.' The final entry, on the 15th, read: '1 p.m. Storm ended. Sea calm. God is over all'

same nonsense over and over again.

In recent years, possibly because of the worldwide attention given to the Bermuda Triangle, the subject of mysterious disappearances has attracted considerable interest and a large number of truly incredible 'vanishings' have been recorded: there is the case of David Lang who vanished before the startled eyes of his family; of the 11-year-old boy who went to fetch a bucket of water from a well and vanished, leaving in the snow a trail of footprints that came to a sudden and abrupt end; of the British diplomat who walked around the heads of his horses and seemingly stepped off the face of the Earth; of an English settlement in North America that disappeared into thin air; of the three lighthouse keepers who vanished from Eilean Mor, off the coast of Scotland, in 1900. Case after amazing case.

James Burne Worson was a shoemaker of

Leamington Spa, Warwickshire, who boasted about his physical prowess and stamina to such a degree that one day in 1873 three of his friends decided to call his bluff and they wagered that he could not run to Coventry and back. Worson accepted the challenge and set off. He jogged down the dusty roads and his friends – Hammerson Burns, Barham Wise, and a third man whose name is not known – followed in a horse-drawn cart, watching Worson carefully for any sign that he was about to give up. Several miles had been covered in this manner when Worson suddenly stumbled. He cried out – and vanished!

This remarkable story has been told in several books, sometimes with a little elaboration, sometimes with a few details omitted, but it is always essentially the same. Rarely is a source given for the story and when one is, it always turns out to be another book about unexplained phenomena. Nobody, it seems, has tried to verify the truth of the tale. Nobody has produced a contemporary newspaper account of the disappearance or a report of the police investigation or of the

All smoke and no fire

One of the more dramatic ways in which people have been known to disappear from this life is by means of spontaneous human combustion. Apparently, 7 April 1938 saw no less than three people engulfed in flames: Willem ten Bruik, who was driving a Volkswagen near Nijmegen, Holland; John Greeley, who was at the wheel of the ss *Ulrich*, approaching Cornwall; and lorry driver George Turner, reportedly burnt to ashes in Chester, though a can of petrol was untouched beside him. Not only that, but the apparent locations of the three deaths make an isosceles triangle.

Unfortunately, Volkswagens were not made at the time, the *Ulrich* does not appear on Lloyd's register, and no George Turner died in Chester that day. The three cases seem to be the product less of fire than of an overheated imagination – in this instance belonging to author Eric Frank Russell, who reports two of them as fact.

Left: Leamington Spa in the mid 19th century. It was from here that James Burne Worson is said to have set out on his run to Coventry in 1873 before disappearing en route. Reliable facts about this story are difficult to find. Indeed, the tale has probably never been verified

Right: Labour MP Victor Grayson addresses a rally in 1906. Grayson, a rousing orator, vanished during a train journey from Liverpool to Hull in 1920. Although there were reports that he had been subsequently seen in Britain and also that he had emigrated to Australia, no final answer has yet been found to the question: what happened to Victor Grayson?

inquest. Nobody has produced any proof of any kind that Worson, Wise and Burns ever lived in Leamington Spa or, indeed, that they ever existed. The only known fact about James Burne Worson is that his death – that is assuming that he was ever born – is *not* recorded at St Catherine's House, repository of all records of births, deaths and marriages filed since 1837.

The story of James Burne Worson is just one of many celebrated cases of 'mysterious' disappearance that have never been substantiated, stories that have been circulating for so long and so widely that authors no more think of checking their veracity than an historian would bother to confirm that the battle of Hastings took place in 1066.

It is sometimes difficult to take a charitable view of the authors who perpetuate these non-mysteries. Some authors have related cases that they clearly know to be fraudulent, others have been satisfied to conduct little or no research beyond borrowing their material from somebody else, many are interested only in amazing their readers and are happy to disregard the facts completely.

The blurb to *Stranger than science* (1963) by the late American writer and broadcaster Frank Edwards says: 'The author has carried out extensive research to establish the authenticity and accuracy of all these fascinating stories.' Edwards says that if asked to cite what he believed to be the strangest case of disappearance he would 'unhesitatingly refer to a twin-engined Marine plane which crashed on the Tahoma Glacier in 1947'. Searchers apparently reached the aircraft and could

tell from the wreckage that the crew could not possibly have survived such a devastating crash, yet not one body of the 32 people who had been on board could be found. The authorities were baffled and offered a reward of $5000 for information leading to the recovery of the bodies.

In fact this aircraft crashed in 1946, not 1947, 10,000 feet (3000 metres) up the storm-shrouded west slope of the crevasse-scored South Tahoma Glacier in the state of Washington, USA. Six months later, on 18 July 1947, searchers eventually reached the crash site and found all the bodies embedded in the ice. Bad weather and dangerous rock falls made recovery too hazardous to contemplate and the corpses lie there to this day. A memorial service was held for the men on 24 August 1947.

The story of how the wreckage was found, the bodies located, and of the memorial service, was told in the *Post-Intelligencer* of

The lady vanishes

In 1937 Amelia Earhart, the celebrated aviator, disappeared in the Pacific during an intended round-the-world flight in a twin-engined Lockheed Elektra. The first woman to have flown the Atlantic solo (and in record time) began her most ambitious journey of all from Miami, accompanied by Fred Noonan, a navigator of great experience.

They headed eastward in a series of planned 'hops'. All went well enough until they left New Guinea. On 2 July at about 7.30 a.m. Earhart radioed that fuel was running low. A little over an hour later she reported her course. She was heading for Howland Island, just north of the equator and east of the Gilbert Islands. Nothing more was heard from her.

The US Navy recorded that the aircraft had been lost at sea. In *The search for Amelia Earhart*, Fred Goerner claims that Earhart was carrying out an intelligence mission, reporting on Japanese military activity, when low fuel and high winds forced her to alter course. He agrees with Admiral Chester Nimitz, former US commander in the Pacific, that the aircraft went down in the Marshall Islands, over which the Japanese held a mandate. Earhart and Noonan may then have been transported to Saipan in the Marianas, for the locals tell of two American fliers, one a woman, who arrived in 1937, were imprisoned and interrogated by the Japanese, and then executed and buried in unmarked graves.

Amelia Earhart and Fred Noonan (above) climb aboard their aircraft in Puerto Rico during their 1937 attempt to fly round the world. They disappeared somewhere between New Guinea and Howland Island (right)

Left: Colonel Percy Fawcett, who disappeared in 1925 in the Amazon jungle

Below: Ambrose Bierce, the American satirist, wrote about mysterious vanishings – and then disappeared himself. Nothing more was heard from him after he went to Mexico in 1913 as an observer with Pancho Villa's rebel army in the civil war

Bottom: South Tahoma Glacier, USA, where an aircraft crashed in 1946 with the loss of 32 lives. The bodies did not vanish, as writer Frank Edwards says; they were found six months later buried in ice

Seattle during August 1947. So much for 'extensive research to establish the authenticity and accuracy . . .'. The only mystery is how the fiction about the bodies being missing survived from 1947 to 1959 when Edwards published his book.

One dark night in November 1878, 16-year-old Charles Ashmore of Quincey, Illinois, went to fetch a pail of water from the well in the yard outside his home. After he had been gone an undue length of time his family went looking for him. In the feeble, flickering light of their lantern they saw the trail of the boy's footprints in the snow, but they came to a sudden and mysterious end halfway to the well. Charles Ashmore had inexplicably vanished. Even more mysterious, for several days Charles's mother could hear her son calling for help.

But wait. Perhaps it was 11-year-old Oliver Larch of South Bend, Indiana, who went to fetch a pail of water on Christmas Eve 1889, and vanished, leaving in the snow a clear trail of footprints, which came to an abrupt end. Or is that Oliver Lerch of the same place who vanished in the same manner on Christmas Eve 1890? Or Oliver Thomas of Rhayader, Wales, who went to fetch a bucket of water on Christmas Eve 1909 and never came back. *His* tracks in the snow ended halfway to the well. Or Charlotte Ashton, who met a similar fate on the night of 17 October 1876. Or James Settle, whose tracks came to an abrupt end in the snow of New York City. One does not have to be a particularly astute reader to detect certain similarities between these stories; perhaps all or some are derivatives of an original. But which account is the original and which, if indeed any, is true?

Ashmore, it seems, was an invention of the writer Ambrose Bierce in one of his short stories. The Oliver Lerch story (the change of year and the name from Larch to Lerch came later) is an old newspaper hoax, and its inconsistencies have been exposed several times: for example, there was no snow in South Bend, Indiana, over the Christmas period in 1890. As for the Welsh boy, Oliver Thomas, the story appears to have originated with a writer who is notorious for fictionalising events. The present author has searched the relevant copies of the *Brecon County Times*, which served the Rhayader area, and discovered that they contain no mention of an Oliver Thomas vanishing. There is also no record of a birth or death certificate for an Oliver Thomas of Rhayader to be found at St Catherine's House. From this we can conclude only that, like Ashmore and Lerch, Oliver Thomas is a figment of somebody's imagination. The same is also true of Charlotte Ashton and James Settle.

Abducted by a UFO?

Several writers have used one or more of these stories to support a particular theory. For example, in his book *Strangers from the skies* (1966), Brad Steiger tells a much-expanded story of the Oliver Thomas 'disappearance' in a chapter called 'Flying saucers and disappearing people'. Steiger does not directly state that Oliver Thomas was abducted by a UFO, but his account follows the question: '. . . have outer-space creatures been periodically plucking up earthlings for study and interrogation?'

In his book *Vanishings*, Michael Harrison speculates whether the boys' cries (Larch and Thomas are supposed to have cried out something like: 'Help! They've got me!' which has, not unnaturally, given rise to much speculation about the use of the plural) released some sort of energy that snatched the boys away. 'Had the three boys remained silent,' writes Harrison, 'there would have been no sound to activate the forces arrayed against them; forces their own fear, *as well as the paraphysical properties of lonely farmhouses*, had created.' (The italics are Harrison's.)

Michael Harrison does not explain what paraphysical properties lonely farmhouses have, but such speculation, be it ludicrous or not – and frequently it can only be politely described as imaginative – is valueless when the incidents on which it is based never happened.

If 'mystery' books – which are presented as fact – are bought for their entertainment value, readers might find their money better spent on horror fiction, in which there is certainly no shortage of suitably blood-chilling tales to set the imagination working overtime of a dark winter night.

Stories of people who 'disappear into thin air' abound – but disappointingly the facts, even in some of the classic cases, do not often bear close scrutiny

IN 1872 THE *Mary Celeste* was found aimlessly wandering in the Atlantic. She was in remarkably good condition and well-provisioned, but her crew had apparently abandoned ship. Since no experienced sailor is ever likely to desert a seaworthy ship for a comparatively dangerous lifeboat unless his life is in severe danger, the disappearance of *Mary Celeste*'s crew is an outstanding mystery (see page 76). Over the years, however, it has been made even more mysterious by the addition of fictional details such as half-eaten breakfasts being found on the galley table and the aroma of fresh tobacco smoke lingering in the captain's cabin.

Such additions come into being for many reasons: to add to the eeriness of a story for entertainment value, for example, or, less innocently, with the deliberate intention of introducing supernatural overtones to a mystery that would otherwise be confined within the comparatively boring limitations of the natural and the known. Another much-publicised case is that of the disappearance in 1809 of the British diplomat Benjamin Bathurst (see page 32).

The Bathurst disappearance is a complex and, indeed, an impenetrable mystery yet, perhaps significantly, it is rarely expanded beyond a single, simple, and mystery-making paragraph that generally goes along the lines of: Benjamin Bathurst was about to board a coach outside an inn in (or near)

Disappearing disappearances

Berlin. He was seen to walk around the heads of the horses – and was never seen again.

The disappearance of Bathurst is far too complex to describe here in anything but the broadest outline, but it is sufficient to say that in 1809 the British government sent him on a secret mission to the Court of Austria. Earlier in the year the Austrians had suffered a demoralising defeat at the hands of Napoleon and it is generally accepted that Bathurst's mission was to dissuade Emperor Francis II from total capitulation.

Bathurst was returning from this mission with a companion when he stopped at an inn in Perleberg, a day's journey from Hamburg, where a ship was waiting to return him to England. He stayed at the inn for a few hours and at 9 p.m. he told his companion that he was going to have the horses made ready for the continuation of the journey. What happened next is disputed. According to the memoirs of his father, Bishop Bathurst, published in 1837, it was an hour before the

One of the most frequently told 'mysterious disappearance' stories is that of the British diplomat Benjamin Bathurst (above), who walked round the heads of his coach horses in the German town of Perleberg (right) in 1809 – and vanished, never to be seen again. His disappearance, however, seems less mysterious when it is known that he was on a top secret political mission at the time

companion grew alarmed by Bathurst's continued absence and made enquiries, learning that Bathurst was about to climb into his coach when something in the shadows of the entrance to the inn courtyard caught his attention and apparently compelled him to investigate. He walked into the darkness and was never seen again.

So it is most certainly a mystery, but there was almost certainly no supernatural element to the Bathurst story. Nobody actually saw Bathurst disappear into thin air. He did *not* simply walk around the heads of his horses and step off the face of the Earth. It should be remembered that Bathurst was in a precarious political position: Napoleon would have been interested in the outcome of Bathurst's discussion with Francis II, and Bathurst had made enemies at the Emperor's court who may not have wished to see a renewal of hostilities between Austria and France. Besides, there were rogues and vagabonds in Perleberg itself who would have killed Bathurst for no more than the clothes he wore. Bathurst could have met his end at the hands of any one of these. Yet the fact remains that his body was never found.

The exciting story of the 'lost colony' is another mystery that some unscrupulous authors have made more mysterious than it ever was, although this time they have done it by omitting certain details. The tale has several versions, a typical account being that given in Michael Harrison's *Vanishings*.

According to Harrison: in 1585 Sir Walter Raleigh established a settlement on Roanoke Island off the coast of present-day North Carolina. Harrison says that Raleigh left the colonists and

> returned to England for needed supplies and a reinforcement of emigrants. The date of the settlement was 1585. When Raleigh returned to Roanoke, he found no trace of the settlers; all had gone. . . . The rationalists say that, despairing of their ever seeing Raleigh again, the settlers trekked over the mainland until they were either captured by, or voluntarily made common cause with, the Mandan Indians.

Almost everything Harrison has written about the disappearance of the Roanoke settlement is wrong. Raleigh organised and part-financed the settlement, but he never visited Roanoke personally. The colony that disappeared did so in or after 1587, not 1585, and the man who returned to England for supplies was not Raleigh but one John White. He was prevented from returning to the New World for the next three years, during which time the colonists are not known to have seen another European face. From these facts alone it is not too difficult to deduce a reasonable explanation for the disappearance of the colony.

In an effort to dismiss contrary and often more prosaic solutions to these 'mysteries',

Top: Michael Harrison, author of *Vanishings* (1981) which repeats many of the popular tales of people who allegedly disappear under 'mysterious' circumstances

Above: Sir Walter Raleigh (1554–1618) who, in 1585 – according to Harrison – established a settlement on Roanoke Island, off the coast of North Carolina. Harrison says that Raleigh returned to discover that the colonists had vanished. Yet the fact is that Raleigh never visited the settlement personally

sensationalist authors employ a variety of writing techniques designed to persuade the reader that the unlikely explanation is in fact the more reasonable one. Harrison uses one of these ploys when he refers to the theory that the colonists were absorbed by the Mandan Indians. He is clearly contemptuous of those whom he calls 'rationalists', implying that the *only* rational solution ever offered is the Mandan theory. Presumably the reader is intended to conclude that this is a desperately contrived idea evoked by people who refuse even to consider a more sinister, but reasonable, solution.

The Mandan solution

In fact, rationalists would be among the first to dismiss the Mandan solution as absurd; it is highly improbable that the colonists would have attempted, let alone survived, a crossing from the Outer Banks of North Carolina to the Mandan Indians of Missouri. Moreover, it is doubtful that the Mandan solution was proposed by historians since they have had a fairly good idea of the colonists' fate for over 400 years.

Before John White left Roanoke he arranged that if the colonists abandoned the settlement they should carve the name of their destination on a stockade post and append a cross if the move was made under duress or in distress. To quote White's own words: 'one of the chiefe trees of postes at the right side of the entrance had the barke taken off, and 5 foote [1.5 metres] from the ground in fayre Capitall letters was graven CROATOAN without any crosse or signe of distresse.'

Yet much mystery has been made of this. In his *Strange people* (1966) Frank Edwards writes: 'It is possible that the word meant little or nothing to the Englishmen who found it. Or if they did recognise it as a clue to the missing colonists, perhaps they realised that they dared not follow the clue to its conclusion.' All very mystery-making – and all very untrue. White had stated quite plainly: 'I greatly joyed that I had safely found a certaine token of their safe being at Croatoan, which is the place where Manteo was borne, and the savages of the Iland our friends.'

White's joy was short-lived. He was prevented from going to Croatoan and was never able to verify that this was where the colonists went, but it is a fair conclusion that without food, surrounded on all sides by hostile Indians, and cut off from home in a new, unexplored, and equally hostile country, the settlers would have sought refuge in the one place where they were assured of friendship – Croatoan. Sad to relate, there is some evidence that suggests that the Indians of Croatoan were later massacred by the Indians of the powerful Powhatan Confederacy of the Algonkian tribes in the Virginia Tidewater.

The Roanoke disappearance *is* a mystery,

but only insofar as there is no absolute proof of the colonists' fate and not because of any suggestion that their disappearance was in even the slightest way paranormal or supernatural.

Another example of the 'manufactured mystery' is the case of the missing Norfolks (see page 68), a battalion of British soldiers who disappeared at Gallipoli in 1915 and whose fate remains unknown to this day – a mystery that considerably pales in significance when one takes into account the fact that 27,000 British and Empire troops died at Gallipoli and have no known grave. However, the story has become particularly popular in books about 'mysterious' disappearances and UFOs because a soldier named Reichardt claimed to have witnessed their fate. He says they were abducted by a cloud.

Delayed reaction

Most accounts of the Norfolk disappearance omit to mention that Reichardt told his story 50 years after the event at an old comrades' reunion – events that are not noted as particularly sober affairs – and that it contains many details that are either wrong or inconsistent with the circumstances of the genuine disappearance. Examined in the light of thoroughly documented facts, it is almost certain that Reichardt confused two separate incidents.

In recent years writers such as Lawrence Kusche, Ronald Story and Philip Klass have conducted thorough research into many fields of the unexplained and on the basis of well-researched, and fully documented, evidence have concluded that many stories such as that of the Norfolks are not supported by the facts. Of course, these conclusions do not have to be accepted, but they should not be dismissed without reason. Some authors, however, for reasons best known to themselves, refuse to accept that certain stories have been demonstrated to be untrue and they continue to repeat these tales without providing a scrap of evidence to support their reasons for having done so. It might be thought that such authors intend deliberately to mislead their readers.

In this respect, two books are noteworthy for the retelling of tales long since discredited: Charles Berlitz's *Without a trace* (1978) and Michael Harrison's *Vanishings* (1981). Charles Berlitz, for instance, repeats once more the story of the *Freya* as a Bermuda Triangle fatality, long after it had been established that the incident took place in the Pacific; and Michael Harrison, while claiming to have read most, if not all, of the books that expose so many of these tales, nevertheless presents them again as if such evidence did not exist, or could safely be ignored.

For example, Harrison dismisses the errors in Reichardt's story about the disappearing Norfolks as 'unimportant' – which they most certainly were not – and makes the

Above: a drawing of the Indian settlement Secoton by John White, the English colonist who discovered the message left by the 'missing' settlers. They quite clearly stated that they were intending to make for the village of Croatoan – yet curiously many popular accounts of the settlers' subsequent disappearance make no mention of this

Above right: a North American Indian, as painted by one of the first European settlers. The Indians at Croatoan were known to be friendly to the Roanoke settlers, but shortly after the Europeans are assumed to have arrived at Croatoan it was overrun by a hostile tribe – and there were few survivors

remarkable statement that Reichardt's story was received by 'sceptics baying for "the facts"'. It seems he expects fantastic tales to be accepted without an ounce of corroborative evidence.

The paranormal attracts frauds, cranks, and hoaxers, and it is never easy to distinguish between serious books about the paranormal and those that are sensationalist. A good rule of thumb guide is to check whether the author begins by appealing to his readers not to have a closed mind.

In the introduction to her book *They dared the Devil's Triangle*, Adi-Kent Thomas Jeffrey almost fanatically implores her readers:

. . . let us lift our faces to the winds of mystery and not cover our senses with the impenetrable armour of suspicion and skepticism. . . . Let us not don the thick-helmet of closed-mindedness under the guise of so-called 'common sense' or 'reason'.

And in the foreword to *Vanishings* Michael Harrison similarly warns his readers against 'contemptuous scoffers' and 'authors charitably inclined to reassure the uneasy'.

But facts speak for themselves. The author of a well-researched and fully documented book has no need so to implore his readers. But the absence of facts is, of course, the essential weakness of writers who seek only to amaze and astound, and what sensationalist writers want of you, apart from your money, is your faith in what they write.

Facts and fictions

Two of the most frequently repeated of all 'mysterious disappearance' stories are those of David Lang and the airliner *Star Tiger*. But it appears that the real mystery is the extent of human credulity

DAVID LANG disappeared on 23 September 1880 in front of five witnesses – or so the story goes. This is probably the most famous case of 'vanishing' on record and the story has been told by so many authors that a list of their names would read like a *Who's who* of writers on matters paranormal. Yet not one of them has produced a scrap of evidence that David Lang ever existed.

Apparently, Lang was walking across the 40-acre (16-hectare) pasture in front of his large, vine-covered farmhouse on the 'Old Cottontown Road' near Gallatin in Sumner County, Tennessee, USA, when a buggy turned into the long drive leading to the house. It contained a friend of the family, Judge August Peck, and his brother-in-law, a man named Wade, from Akron, Ohio. Lang waved and began to retrace his steps to the house. He had gone no more than a short distance when he vanished. One moment he was there, the next he was gone. David Lang had stepped off the face of the earth. Mrs Lang, the two Lang children, Judge Peck and his brother-in-law had all seen farmer David Lang cease to exist.

Events were to become even more bizarre. About a year later the Lang children, Sarah and George, noticed that there was a ring of stunted yellow grass on the spot where David Lang had vanished. For some reason Sarah called her father's name and to her astonishment received a faint reply. Her father called for help over and over again until eventually his voice faded away for ever.

Years later Sarah Lang developed an interest in Spiritualism and, according to an article entitled 'How lost was my father' in *Fate* magazine (July 1953), which was written by Stuart Palmer but based on Sarah Lang's own testimony, she spent thousands

Below: Herbert Hoover, then US Secretary of Commerce, headed the investigation into the mysterious disappearance of the *Carroll A. Deering* (bottom). The ship had been found drifting in 1921. There was no sign of life but no evidence of bloodshed or violence. Three months later one Christopher Gray of North Carolina claimed to have found a dramatic message in a bottle that stated that the crew had been kidnapped, but Hoover dismissed it as Gray's own work. The fate of the ship

of dollars cultivating the most famous mediums, but with little success. Then someone gave her a planchette – an automatic writing device – and this awakened her own psychic abilities. In April 1929, compelled by a strange force to take up her planchette, Sarah Lang received the message: 'Together now and forever . . . after many years . . . God bless you.' Sarah compared this 'spirit' writing with an inscription written by her father on the flyleaf of a book. The writing matched. Sarah knew that at long last her father and mother were reunited in the realm beyond the grave.

Sarah Lang speaks out
The story of David Lang contains three elements, the last of which – Sarah's story as told to Stuart Palmer – would help to confirm the others, so let us examine it first.

Palmer sent his article with a covering letter to Curtis Fuller, editor of *Fate*, and by good fortune that letter remained in the magazine's files. In it Palmer says that the article is a rewrite of a story he had written years before for *Ghost*, a small magazine published in 1936 and 1937. As proof of the truth of the story, Palmer and Sarah Lang went to the trouble of signing an affidavit and having it witnessed by a notary public. Palmer concludes the *Fate* article by saying: 'a student of Clark Sellers, perhaps the nation's foremost expert in handwriting and the study of questioned documents, has said that the inscription on Miss Lang's childhood book and the planchette writing are by the same hand.'

It is worthwhile noting that neither the handwriting expert nor Palmer says that the handwriting was that of Sarah Lang's father. A researcher and writer named Robert Schadewald submitted reproductions of the handwriting in the book, the planchette writing and the signatures on the affidavit to Ann B. Hooten, a member of the prestigious American Society of Document Examiners. Miss Hooten's reply came in the form of a

five-page report in which she concluded that the result of her examination conclusively proved that the accumulated writings were from the same individual. In other words, David and Sarah Lang's handwriting is, by some strange 'coincidence', the same as Stuart Palmer's.

Hershel G. Payne, a librarian at the Public Library of Nashville and Davidson County, was intrigued by the celebrated local mystery and set out to establish as many facts about it as he could. He checked the census records for 1830, 1850 and 1880, but there was no mention of anyone named Lang or Peck. He consulted a dozen or more early histories of the area, but none of them mentioned Lang or the Lang farm. Other librarians, local newspapers and local historians all replied to his requests with the same answer: there were no documents, photographs or records of any kind attesting to Lang, Peck or the Lang farm. Mr Payne even drove down the 'Old Cottontown Road', but found nothing that could have been or may once have been the Lang farm.

Numerous writers have told this story and each has used an earlier writer as their source. The principal source since the 1960s has been Frank Edwards's book *Stranger than science*, or books that have used

> To Whom It May Concern:
>
> I, Sarah Emma Lang, hereby affirm and depose that I have read the accompanying hitherto unpublished account of my father, David Lang's, disappearance, and that in every detail this story is true.
>
> Signed *Sarah Emma Lang*
>
> Witnessed by *Stuart Palmer*
>
> Subscribed and sworn to before me this 30th day of October, 1929 *William C Kimberley*
>
> Notary Public in and for the County of New York, State of New York.
>
> My Commission expires March 30, 1931

The extraordinary collection of 'evidence' for the Lang case: Sarah Lang and author Stuart Palmer swore an affidavit (above) to the effect that the story of David Lang's 'disappearance' is true; and the two samples of handwriting, one taken from the flyleaf of a book (below left) and the other allegedly written from beyond the grave (below) by means of a planchette (bottom). Handwriting experts agreed that the samples were written by the same person – but further research revealed that that person was Stuart Palmer, whose article for *Fate* magazine popularised the story

*To Sarah:—
On her tenth birthday,
From
her Father*

*together now and
forever
after many years God bless you*

Edwards's information. Edwards does not give his source, but it could have been any one of a number of writers who cite one of two articles about the Lang 'disappearance' in *Fate*: either that written by the psychical researcher Nandor Fodor, which was published in December 1956, or Stuart Palmer's article of July 1953. Palmer, of course, was rewriting his article originally written for *Ghost*, and it is at this point that the trail to the origin of the story runs into a stone wall. On the other side of the wall the trail picks up in 1893 with the publication of *Can such things be?* by Ambrose Bierce, which features a story called 'The difficulty of crossing a

field', based on the Lang case.

Bierce is believed to have taken the idea from an article in the *Cincinnati Enquirer*, but the date of publication is unknown; copies of the newspaper for the 1880s are available on microfilm, but there is no index and searches have failed to locate the relevant edition. However, the article is thought to have been written by a travelling salesman named Joe Mulhatten from Cincinnati who was delayed in Gallatin, Tennessee, by a snowstorm in 1889, and wrote the tale to pass the time and earn a few extra dollars. But where did he get the story?

The biggest lie of all

Hershel G. Payne says that in the late 1880s there were lying contests, a prize being awarded to whoever told the biggest lie. Mulhatten apparently won with his story of David Lang. However, in his book *Among the missing*, Jay Robert Nash says that the Lang story was based on a real event: the disappearance in July 1854 of Orion Williamson from his farm in Selma, Alabama. And so we are back to square one. Did Orion Williamson vanish?

The story of the search to verify the 'mystery' of David Lang serves to illustrate how such myths are born and how they develop over the years as they pass from one author to another, are occasionally elaborated, and sometimes even gain fraudulent 'corroborative evidence'. In the end the story becomes so well-accepted as fact that nobody thinks to check it, or perhaps they choose not to. For example, the Lang case crops up in *Vanishings* by Michael Harrison (1981) – despite the fact that at least one of the sources quoted gives all the information you have just read.

It is, perhaps, disappointing when such tales turn out to be no more than fiction, but some people – writers and readers alike – are so wrapped up in self-deception that they are hostile to any suggestion that these cherished whimsies are anything other than fact.

It may be argued that the truth of such

called Station VRT, and no radio message was dispatched from the aircraft at 10.30 p.m.

None of these errors is particularly important insofar as they influence either Wolfe's theories or provide any possible solutions to the airliner's fate, but it is worth considering whether any rational reader would tolerate a history book that claimed that the battle of Hastings was a fist fight between Robin Hood and Abraham Lincoln. The mistakes made by many writers of books about the unexplained are of this calibre.

Often there is no deliberate intent to deceive and errors do not always invalidate the rest of an article or book, but it is a rather

Above: in 1858, 650 highly trained French troops, sent to quell a riot in the Indo-Chinese city of Saigon, apparently disappeared only 15 miles (24 kilometres) from their destination. Did they desert *en masse*, were they taken prisoner or blown up – or was there a genuine mystery involved?

stories is irrelevant because they are read for their entertainment value, but people do honestly believe these tales or at least believe that there is some substance behind them. Children are particularly susceptible to the misconceptions promoted through sensationalist books, and teachers have frequently expressed their concern over them.

James Raymond Wolfe contributed a chapter to *The riddle of the Bermuda Triangle* edited by Martin Ebon. Wolfe is a lecturer in paranormal phenomena at Clark University in Worcester, Massachusetts, USA, and his chapter, says Ebon, was 'edited from a segment of one of his course lectures'. In other words, this is what he told his students.

Referring to the *Star Tiger*, an airliner that disappeared on a flight from the Azores to Bermuda Wolfe says: 'At 10.30 p.m. its pilot, Captain David Colby, radioed the tower at Hamilton, Bermuda. . . .' Hardly one of these 13 words is correct. The pilot was Captain Brian McMillan (Colby was the First Officer), all radio messages were sent by Robert Tuck and were not sent to the tower at Hamilton but to an Air Guard service

Above: in 1889 Malcolm Macmillan, a publisher from London and forbear of Harold Macmillan (the former British Prime Minister), vanished from the summit of Mount Hymettus in Greece. He had paused to wave to some companions, then disappeared. Careful searches of the area gave no hint as to his fate, yet the possibility remains that he could have committed suicide, his body being concealed by undergrowth

disturbing thought that parts of one's general knowledge are completely untrue. That is one of the reasons why stories such as that of David Lang have to be weeded out and set aside.

Critics of the many sensationalist books and their writers lay themselves open to the accusation of being unwilling to accept anything that lies outside the bounds of orthodoxy. But such criticism is not indicative of having a closed mind. On the contrary, it indicates having an open mind, one that is prepared to accept the possible truth that David Lang vanished before the startled eyes of his family and friends, but also a mind willing to investigate the story and try to get at the truth.

People do disappear and sometimes in the most bizarre circumstances. It remains possible that some people have stepped into another dimension or have been snatched by a UFO or fallen into a timeless void, but no matter how fascinating or frightening such possibilities might be, they remain the province of science fantasy writers until good, hard evidence can be presented to support their possible reality.

The day the Norfolks disappeared

One of the most frequently repeated stories of mysterious disappearances concerns an entire Norfolk regiment – allegedly abducted by a UFO in 1915. PAUL BEGG examines the story in the light of new evidence

THERE ARE MANY STRANGE accounts of people having been abducted by a UFO. In most cases the unfortunate victim is returned to Earth and able to tell his story, often to an incredulous audience who not unnaturally express considerable disbelief. But sometimes the victim disappears forever, his fate to remain unknown. These cases are rare because a number of witnesses are required if more prosaic explanations for the disappearance are to be dismissed. Of this latter category is the case of the vanishing Norfolks, one of the most bizarre of such incidents and accordingly featured in dozens of books about UFOs, the Bermuda Triangle, and other 'paranormal' mysteries. But is it – can it possibly be – true?

The incident allegedly took place in August 1915 during the ill-fated Gallipoli campaign. According to a statement made by three of the original witnesses, 22 members of a New Zealand field company saw a large number of British soldiers, later identified as the 'First-Fourth Norfolk Regiment', march into a strange loaf-of-bread shaped cloud that was straddling a dry creek bed. After the last man had entered, the cloud lifted and moved off *against* the wind. Not one of the soldiers was ever seen again.

The New Zealanders' story contained

Below: troops landing at Anzac Cove, Gallipoli, in 1915. Conditions were appalling; dysentery decimated the ranks and corpses lay everywhere, adding to the nightmare

some obvious errors; the First-Fourth Norfolk was not a regiment, for example, but a battalion of the Royal Norfolk Regiment. None of the errors has ever been corrected in any of the books that feature the story, which suggests that it has never been substantiated, the authors having simply copied the myth from one another.

This opinion is supported by one further and very important fact: the First-Fourth Norfolk did not disappear from Gallipoli in August 1915 or at any time or place thereafter. There is ample evidence to show that

they were in active service until the end of the year, when they were withdrawn from Gallipoli and sent to another theatre of war.

This fact would be sufficient to dispose of the New Zealanders' story of cosmic abduction as a figment of someone's imagination, but, perhaps coincidentally, it is a matter of undisputed historical fact that another battalion of the Royal Norfolk Regiment, the First-Fifth, *did* disappear at Gallipoli in August 1915, their fate never having been satisfactorily ascertained. Therefore, if the New Zealanders saw any Norfolks abducted, those Norfolks could only have been the First-Fifth. So is it possible that, bizarre though their story most certainly is, 22 members of a New Zealand field company did witness the fate of the First-Fifth Norfolk? If not, where did their story come from, and what was the First-Fifth's fate?

The twisting trail in search of some answers begins in Dereham, a small market town not far from Norwich, England. It was here, as part of the predominantly East Anglian 163rd Brigade, that the First-Fourth and First-Fifth Norfolks prepared to go to war.

They were Territorials – called 'Saturday night soldiers' by men of the regular army – but they belonged to a regiment with a long and distinguished history going back to 1685, when it was raised by King James II at the time of Monmouth's Rebellion. At that time it was called Colonel Henry Cornwall's 9th Regiment of Foot.

The Norfolks embarked for Gallipoli on 29 July 1915. The Gallipoli campaign was fought for control of the Dardanelles – the ancient Hellespont – a long, narrow channel extending some 40 miles (65 kilometres) along the Gallipoli Peninsula in Turkey and

Below: a corner of the ANZAC position. Digging in was a necessary evil in a slow-moving war, providing both shelter and cover. But the overcrowding and less than perfect sanitation, added to the heat and flies, meant a squalid death for many before they had fired a shot. It was in such chaotic conditions that the Norfolks 'disappeared'

Bottom: Turkish artillery pound the ANZACS during the advance on Tekke and Kavak Tepe

connecting the Mediterranean with the Black Sea, for which reason it had acquired strategic importance following the alliance between Turkey and Germany.

The Gallipoli Peninsula is exquisitely beautiful in spring and early summer, but from May onwards it bakes under a relentless sun and by August it is one of the most inhospitable places on Earth. It was on 10 August, at the height of the terrible summer, that the Norfolks landed at Suvla Bay and surveyed what had already become the graveyard for so many men.

Not far from the beach was a large salt lake. Dry in summer, it reflected the harsh glare of the sun. Beyond lay the battlefield, Suvla Plain, and in the distance a semicircle of bleak hills stretched from north to south,

giving the plain the appearance of a giant arena. The northernmost was Kiretch Tepe, in the middle were the twin heights of Kavak Tepe and Tekke Tepe, and to the south was Sari Bair.

The Gallipoli campaign has gone down as one of the worst theatres of war in recent military history and to those Norfolks who had deluded themselves that they were off on a great adventure, the sights that met their eyes must have seemed like a nightmare vision of hell.

Conditions were appalling. The trenches were like ovens; a hot wind, pungent with the stench of death, stirred a fine dust across the plain; the food, the trenches, the latrines and the corpses were infested with a vile, bloated green fly – called the 'corpse fly' by the men because it feasted on the bodies of the dead and wounded – that spread a particularly virulent form of dysentery from which no soldier escaped and that reduced many to walking skeletons.

The troops, riddled with disease, were exhausted; corpses lay about in great numbers and it was by no means unusual to see the face or hands of a hastily buried comrade protruding from the ground; morale was low and a miasma of defeat hung heavy in the air.

The Norfolks had no experience of combat and in normal circumstances they would have been given time to acclimatise in a quiet sector, but Sir Ian Hamilton, Commander-in-Chief of the Mediterranean Expeditionary Force, believed that the only chance of wresting victory from the jaws of dreadful defeat lay in the use of his fresh forces in a major offensive.

Into the jaws of death

Hamilton envisaged a bold, sweeping attack on Tekke and Kavak Tepe and it was arranged that under cover of darkness on the night of 12 August the 54th Division (of which the Norfolks' brigade was a part) should advance to the foothills and prepare to attack at dawn the next day. However, it was believed that a cultivated area called Kuchuk Anafarta Ova, over which the night advance would take place, was held by enemy snipers and it was accordingly decided that the Norfolks' 163rd Brigade should move forward and clear the area during the afternoon of 12 August.

The advance that afternoon was a complete and utter fiasco, a prime example of the muddle and incompetence that marked the whole Gallipoli campaign. It was to begin at 4 p.m. with artillery support, but there was a delay of 45 minutes; however faulty communications prevented the artillery from being informed and they opened fire as scheduled, thereby wasting their support. The area was totally unreconnoitred, commanding officers were unfamiliar with the terrain and uncertain about their objective, most of the maps hurriedly issued at the last moment only depicted another part of the

Top: the 'glorious fallen'. The effects of delay in burial and the burning heat made identification of the corpses often impossible

Above: Major-General Sir Ian Hamilton, Commander-in-Chief of the Mediterranean Expeditionary Force, under whose command 46,000 men lost their lives – including the 267 men of the Norfolks

Peninsula, and the strength of the enemy was completely unknown.

The 163rd Brigade, with the First-Fourth Norfolk bringing up the rear, had advanced no more than about 1000 yards (900 metres) when it became obvious that a mistake had been made in trying to cross the open plain in daylight. The strength of the enemy was greater than had been supposed and the main body of the brigade encountered heavy machine-gun fire and were forced to ground. However, on the right flank the First-Fifth Norfolk encountered less stiff opposition and pressed forward.

Sir Ian Hamilton described the following events in a dispatch to Lord Kitchener, the Secretary of State for War:

In the course of the fight, creditable in all respects to the 163rd Brigade, there happened a very mysterious thing . . . Against the yielding forces of the enemy Colonel Sir H. Beauchamp, a bold, self-confident officer, eagerly pressed forward, followed by the best part of the battalion. The fighting grew hotter, and the ground became more wooded and broken. At this stage many men were wounded or grew exhausted with thirst. These found their way back to camp during the night. But the Colonel, with 16 officers and 250 men, still kept pushing forward, driving the enemy before him. . . . Nothing more was seen or heard of any of them. They charged into the forest and were lost to sight or sound. Not one of them ever came back.

Two hundred and sixty-seven men had vanished without trace!

The failure of the advance that afternoon delivered a crushing blow to Sir Ian Hamilton's hope of turning the tide of the campaign and the evacuation of Allied forces at the end of 1915 was a major defeat. The Gallipoli campaign had lasted eight and a half months and cost the lives of about 46,000 soldiers, a horrific number by any previous standards of modern warfare. In 1916 the Government appointed a Royal Commission to investigate the causes of the defeat. A heavily censored report, *The final report of the Dardanelles commission*, was released in 1917 and another in 1919. It was not until 1965 that a declassified edition was made available – a significant date as we shall see.

The fate of the First-Fifth Norfolk remained a mystery for four years when there was a further development in the story.

At the end of 1918 the British returned to

Above: a poster celebrating the Turkish victory over the invading ANZAC forces, Gallipoli, 1915

Below: Turkish troops. Knowing the terrain, used to the climate and far better organised, their victory over the ANZAC troops rapidly became inevitable

Gallipoli as the ultimate victors. A soldier of the Occupation Forces was touring the battlefield when he found a cap badge of the Royal Norfolk Regiment, and on making enquiries he learned that a Turkish farmer had removed a large number of bodies from his property and dumped them in a nearby ravine. On 23 September 1919, following the unpleasant task of recovering the bodies, an officer commanding a Graves Registration Unit triumphantly announced:

We have found the Fifth Norfolk – there were 180 in all: 122 Norfolk and a few Hants and Suffolks with 2/4th Cheshires. We could only identify two – Privates Barnaby and Carter. They were scattered over an area of about one square mile [3 square kilometres], at a distance of at least 800 yards [750 metres] behind the Turkish front line. Many of them had evidently been killed in a farm, as a local Turk, who owns the land, told us that when he came back he found the farm covered with the decomposing bodies of British soldiers which he threw into a small ravine. The whole thing quite bears out the original theory that they did not go very far on, but got mopped up one by one, all except the ones who got into the farmhouse.

'We have found the Fifth Norfolk . . . Although generally considered the last word on the fate of the First-Fifth Norfolk, it is evident that this statement was somewhat premature. Only 122 Norfolks were found, which leaves more than half the men who vanished unaccounted for. Their fate remains a mystery – unless, of course, the New Zealanders' story of the strange cloud is true.

Lost, believed kidnapped

Fifty years after the Gallipoli campaign three old soldiers came forward with a bizarre tale of a cloud kidnapping a whole regiment. The timing of their accounts shed new light on this 'mysterious' disappearance

ON 12 AUGUST 1915 the best part of the First-Fifth Battalion of the Royal Norfolk Regiment disappeared. The decomposing corpses of slightly less than half the battalion were later found, but the precise fate of the remaining troops remains a mystery. However, a solution may lie in a story which has featured in several books about UFOs and other relative phenomena. According to a statement made by three of the original witnesses, members of a New Zealand field company saw a large number of British troops abducted by a strange cloud, perhaps a UFO. The troops were identified as the First-Fourth Norfolk and the event allegedly happened on 21 August. As there is ample proof that the First-Fourth Norfolk did not disappear it seems that the New Zealanders' story is either a complete fabrication or describes the fate of another body of men, perhaps the disappearance of the First-Fifth Norfolk on 12 August.

What the New Zealanders allegedly saw is described in a statement signed by three of the original witnesses:

August 21, 1915
The following is an account of the strange incident that happened on the

Below: British troops go 'over the top' during the Gallipoli campaign, 1915. These soldiers were part of the hastily formed Naval division – basically sailors, they lacked proper training in land fighting. Other divisions deployed at Gallipoli were equally inadequately trained. The Norfolks, for example, consisted mainly of raw recruits and 'Saturday soldiers' (Territorials) whose exposure to the conditions at Gallipoli came as a brutal – and in many cases, fatal – shock

above date, which occurred in the morning during the severest and final period of fighting which took place on Hill 60, Suvla Bay, ANZAC.

The day broke clear, without a cloud in sight, as any beautiful Mediterranean day could be expected to be. The exception, however, was a number of perhaps six or eight 'loaf of bread' shaped clouds – all shaped exactly alike – which were hovering over Hill 60. It was noticed that, in spite of a four- or five-mile-an-hour [6–8 km/h] breeze from the south, these clouds did not alter their position in any shape or form, nor did they drift away under the influence of the breeze. They were hovering at an elevation of about 60 degrees as seen from our observation point 500 feet [150 metres] up. Also stationary and resting on the ground right underneath this group of clouds was a similar cloud in shape, measuring about 800 feet [245 metres] in length, 220 feet [65 metres] in height, and 200 feet [60 metres] in width. This cloud was absolutely dense, solid looking in structure, and positioned about 14 to 18 chains [900–1100 metres] from the fighting in British-held territory. All this was observed by twenty-two men of No 3 Section, No 1 Field Company, N.Z.E., including myself, from our trenches on Rhododendron Spur, approximately 2500 yards [1350 metres]

south-west of the cloud on the ground. Our vantage point was overlooking Hill 60 by about 300 feet [90 metres]. As it turned out later, this singular cloud was straddling a dry creek bed or sunken road [Kaiajik Dere] and we had a perfect view of the cloud's sides and ends as it rested on the ground. Its colour was a light grey, as was the colour of the other clouds.

A British regiment, the First-Fourth Norfolk, of several hundred men, was then noticed marching up this sunken road or creek towards Hill 60. However, when they arrived at this cloud, they marched straight into it, with no hesitation, but no one ever came out to deploy and fight at Hill 60. About an hour later, after the last of the file had disappeared into it, this cloud very unobtrusively lifted off the ground and, like any cloud or fog would, rose slowly until it joined the other similar clouds which were mentioned at the beginning of this account. On viewing them again, they all looked alike 'as peas in a pod'. All this time, the group of clouds had been hovering in the same place, but as soon as the singular cloud had risen to their level, they all moved away northwards, i.e. towards Thrace [Bulgaria]. In a matter

Above: seen from a distance the Allied camp at Walkers Ridge, Gallipoli, looks organised enough. But the truth was very different; the tents provided little shelter from the relentless heat for men already weakened by disease

of about three-quarters of an hour they had all disappeared from view.

The regiment mentioned was posted as missing or 'wiped out' and on Turkey surrendering in 1918, the first thing Britain demanded of Turkey was the return of this regiment. Turkey replied that she had neither captured this regiment, nor made contact with it, and did not know it existed. A British Regiment in 1914–18 consisted of any number between 800 and 4000 men. Those who observed this incident vouch for the fact that Turkey never captured that regiment, nor made contact with it.

We, the undersigned, although late in time, this is the 50th Jubilee of the ANZAC landing, declare that the above described incident is true in every word.

Signed by witnesses:
4/165 Sapper F. Reichardt,
    Matata, Bay of Plenty
13/416 Sapper R. Newnes
    157 King Street, Cambridge
J. L. Newman
    75 Freyberg Street, Octumoctai,
    Tauranga
This statement is sometimes accompanied by an extract referring to the event from an

unspecified 'official history' of the Gallipoli campaign:

> They were swallowed up by an unseasonable fog. This fog reflected the sun's rays in such a way that artillery observers were dazzled by its brilliance and unable to fire in support. The two hundred and fifty men were never seen or heard from again.

The New Zealanders' statement contains several obvious errors: ANZAC was not a place at the time (although there is a faint likelihood that they were referring to an area that was invested with that name), but an acronym for Australia and New Zealand Army Corps, and the First-Fourth Norfolk was a battalion of the Royal Norfolk Regiment and not itself a regiment. It is difficult to believe that anyone familiar with the British Army or the Gallipoli campaign would have made such mistakes, which suggests that the statement may have been written by someone other than those who signed it and that signatures were provided without the statement having first been checked for accuracy.

Most important, of course, is the fact that the First-Fourth Norfolk did not disappear but were in active service throughout the Gallipoli campaign. The only Norfolks who disappeared were the First-Fifth Battalion and they disappeared on 12 August, not 21. It is perhaps possible but highly unlikely that the First-Fifth, disorientated after the fighting, wandered around Suvla Plain for nine days, but a more likely explanation for the difference of dates – assuming that the New Zealanders' story relates to the First-Fifth – is that Sapper Reichardt, who seems responsible for telling the story, confused the dates. After all 21 is the reverse of 12.

An insubstantial cloud

As for the substance of Reichardt's story, the most dilligent research has failed to locate any account of the 'kidnapping cloud' predating the signed statement (except the alleged entry in an 'official history', of which more will be said later), and the statement is not contemporary with the events it describes, having been signed at an old comrades' reunion to celebrate the 50th anniversary of the ANZAC landing, namely in 1965. One can only wonder why Mr Reichardt and his companions did not report such an unusual occurrence at the time, or at least when the mystery could not be solved later, but perhaps they feared ridicule. Whatever the reason, the story rests with the testimony of those who signed the statement.

Sapper Frederick Reichardt, a sailor, enlisted in the British Section of the New Zealand Expeditionary Force on 8 October 1914 as a member of No 3 Section, First Divisional Field Company, New Zealand Engineers. He embarked for Gallipoli on 12 April 1915.

It will be recalled that Suvla Plain is dominated by a semicircle of hills stretching from north to south, the southernmost being Sari Bair, which has three summits: Koja Cheman Tepe, Besim Tepe, and Chunuk Bair. The most practical route to the summit of Chunuk Bair is along the Rhododendron Spur, so named by the Allies because of the red flowers (not rhododendrons) that had blazed along its length during the early days of the campaign. It was from Rhododendron Spur that Reichardt claims to have seen the First-Fourth abducted.

One and a half miles (2.5 kilometres) to the north of Chunuk Bair is a small hillock called Hill 60, towards which Reichardt claims the troops were marching when abducted by the cloud. A further three miles (5 kilometres) to the north is Kuchuk Anafarta Ova, the scene of the Norfolks' advance on 12 August.

According to the *War diary* of the First Divisional Field Company, No 3 Section was

Below: a rough trench congested with walking wounded and stretcher cases after an action. Rudimentary medical attention patched up the wounded until they could be carried out to the hospital ships moored offshore. However, the heat and dust – and the ever-present 'corpse fly' – combined to produce fever and infection, which wiped out thousands of the wounded

Right. Turkish attendants look after graves in one of the 31 cemeteries maintained on the Gallipoli Peninsula by the Commonwealth War Graves Commission. Thousands of the dead, however, were never identified and many soldiers were never found

Below: a grim relic of the Gallipoli campaign – a human jawbone washed up by the Aegean Sea 50 years after the Dardanelles invasion by the Allies. Such was the carnage that the tides are still washing up fragments of the fallen and their equipment

three miles (5 kilometres) away from where the Fifth Norfolk vanished and has them marching towards enemy territory; he calls ANZAC a place; he waited 50 years before telling his story. It all weighs against believing the main substance of his story.

The only thing that will tip the scales in his favour is the reference to the event in the unspecified 'official history' of the Gallipoli campaign.

None of the official histories contains the entry cited in connection with Reichardt's story. However, in *The final report of the Dardanelles commission*, on the page facing the account of the First-Fifth's advance on 12 August, is the following:

> By some freak of nature Suvla Bay and Plain were wrapped in a strange mist on the afternoon of 21 August. This was sheer bad luck as we had reckoned on the enemy's gunners being blinded by the declining sun and upon the Turks' trenches being shown up by the evening sun with singular clearness. Actually, we could hardly see the enemy lines this afternoon, whereas to the westward targets stood out in strong relief against the luminous light.

Havoc in the afternoon

There can be no doubt that this is the extract used to support Reichardt's story. And it refers to events on 21 August 1915!

'Freak of nature', 'strange mist', 'luminous light', these are words to conjure with, but the report in fact describes an unseasonable but otherwise perfectly normal mist that descended shortly after noon on 21 August and caused havoc with what was, in terms of numbers, the greatest offensive ever launched at Gallipoli.

During that afternoon a composite ANZAC force of 3000 men attacked Hill 60. The battle would rage for a week before the Allies withdrew, leaving a corpse-strewn hillock behind them. It was in the late afternoon when, as the *Final report* says, the mist reflected the sun. The Sherwood Rangers, led by Sir John Milbanke VC, could not see the enemy, but the enemy could see the Rangers only too well and wiped them out.

It is this incident that Reichardt seems to have confused with the disappearance of the First-Fifth Norfolk to produce the story of the kidnapping cloud. Both incidents are described on facing pages in the *Final report* and significantly, the declassified edition of the report was released in 1965, the same year that Reichardt told his story. But the Norfolks' fate is still a mystery and in all probability will remain one, but it is up to you to decide how mysterious their disappearance is. People disappear in time of war. Of the 34,000 British and Empire troops who died at Gallipoli, 27,000 have no known grave. In the light of such widespread carnage, how many more 'strange disappearances' do those bald statistics hide?

away from the Rhododendron Spur until 13 August, being transferred there on that date. This being the case, Reichardt and his companions were in no position to observe the Norfolks advance in the afternoon of 12 August. However, it is possible that No 3 Section was moved to the Spur during 12 August in order to begin work there at dawn the following day. Reichardt could have had an unimpeded view of the Norfolks' advance, but he was at least four and a half miles (7 kilometres) away and must have had acute powers of observation if he could accurately see what was happening at such a distance and in the midst of a battle.

Sadly, Reichardt's position neither proves nor disproves his story since he says that the troops were marching towards Hill 60, some three miles (5 kilometres) to the south of the scene of the Norfolks' advance. So once again the question is raised as to whether the Norfolks, disorientated, blindly wandered around Suvla Plain for up to nine days, eventually finding themselves heading for Hill 60, which was, incidentally, held by the enemy. This is possible, of course, but it seems highly unlikely that the Norfolks would not have fallen into the hands of either the Allies or the enemy.

When considering this eventuality it is impossible not to balance it against the errors in Reichardt's story: he names the wrong battalion; he calls it a regiment; he gives the date of 21 August, nine days after the First-Fifth disappeared; he says the troops were

The last of the Romanovs?

**The young woman who had been fished out of a Berlin canal claimed to be the Grand Duchess Anastasia, daughter of the last tsar of Russia. Had she really survived the killing of the Imperial Romanovs?
FRANK SMYTH investigates**

ON THE MORNING OF 18 February 1920 the Berlin police issued a bulletin to the press:

> Yesterday evening at 9 p.m. a girl of about twenty jumped off the Bendler Bridge into the Landwehr Canal with the intention of taking her own life. She was saved by a police sergeant and admitted to the Elisabeth Hospital in Lützowstrasse. No papers or valuables of any kind were found in her possession, and she refused to make any statement about herself or her motives for attempting suicide.

As a news item it was trivial enough in a city swarming with despairing refugees, made homeless and stateless by the First World War. As an historical document, however, it may be momentous. For many authorities claim that it records the survival of a young woman who was said to have died with her family in a hail of Bolshevik bullets some 18 months before: Her Imperial Highness the Grand Duchess Anastasia Nikolayevna Romanova, daughter of Nicholas II, the last tsar of Russia.

That would-be suicide, who was known to her neighbours in the affluent university town of Charlottesville, Virginia, USA, as Anna Manahan, lived into her eighties and died in early 1984. She had married Dr John

Below: Tsar Nicholas II, the last Imperial ruler of Russia, and his family. The Romanovs were all believed to have been killed after the Bolshevik revolution – but an amazing story of survival came to light with the sudden appearance of a young woman who said she was Anastasia (third from right), youngest of the daughters

Manahan, a former professor of history at the University of Virginia, in 1967, in order to establish American citizenship. Dr Manahan, who was almost 30 years her junior, not only helped her gain citizenship but also protected her from unwelcome publicity. His very name was a shield to a great extent, for under her previous name of Anna Anderson, which she adopted in the 1920s, she became the subject of two feature films, numerous books and countless articles. She was also the focus of the longest legal case of the 20th century, which ran spasmodically from 1938 until 1970 and was still unresolved by the early 1980s.

Each of the two opposing parties in the court case is made up largely of British and German cousins of the Russian Romanov family. They have fought to establish or refute Anna's claim to be Anastasia – and feelings have run extremely high. For example, when the BBC proposed a television programme on the case in 1958, the late Lord

Mountbatten, a first cousin of the 'real' Anastasia, personally intervened with the then Director General – and the project was cancelled. Lord Mountbatten referred to Anna Anderson as 'the impostor' but at the last hearing of the case before the Federal Supreme Court in Karlsruhe, West Germany, in 1970, the five-member panel of judges used no such term. They upheld earlier decisions that the onus of proving her identity lay with Anna, and that she had failed to do so satisfactorily. They also said that 'the death of Anastasia . . . cannot with absolute certainty be shown to be conclusively proved.'

The last known facts about Grand Duchess Anastasia and her family date from July 1918 and trickled out from the mining town of Ekaterinburg (now Sverdlovsk) in the eastern foothills of the Ural Mountains, where the group had arrived in April 1918. Early the previous year, Russia had erupted in violent revolution, and Nicholas, last of the absolutist Romanov tsars, had abdicated in March 1917. The provisional government – a coalition of members of the old Duma, the former puppet parliament, and the new left-wing revolutionaries – took over. Immediately, the family were made prisoners, presumably for their own safety.

For a few months their imprisonment was nothing more than house arrest at one of their palaces just south of St Petersburg (now Leningrad), but then they were moved to Tobolsk in Siberia.

Following the October Revolution when the Bolsheviks under Lenin came to power, the Tsar and his family were moved to their last known location, the commandeered home of a Professor Nikolai Ipatiev at Ekaterinburg. There they were kept for eight weeks, behind specially built fences with about 50 armed guards.

Externally, Russia still faced attack by the Allies. Internally, the Bolsheviks still had to reckon with the 'White' Russians who were faithful to the old regime.

Indeed, the Bolshevik garrison at Ekaterinburg was beginning to panic by July 1918 when a strong White contingent was moving towards the town. On 4 July, apparently on instructions from Lenin's headquarters in Moscow, the raggle taggle guards at the Ipatiev House were replaced by a smaller and more disciplined force. On 16 July, as the anti-Communist White forces drew into battle positions around Ekaterinburg, an early curfew was imposed. And that night, according to standard history books, the Imperial family vanished for ever.

The official statement of the Bolsheviks said that the Tsar had been shot on the orders of the Ural Oblast Soviet governing Ekaterinburg, and that the rest of the family had been 'evacuated under guard'. This announcement was made in the two or three

Above: Lord Mountbatten, the 'real' Anastasia's cousin. He was uncompromising in his opposition to Anna Anderson's claim to be Anastasia, and once put pressure on the BBC to cancel a proposed television programme about her

Below: Ekaterinburg (now Sverdlovsk) in 1918. The Romanovs were said to have been put to death in this Urals town

days following the family's disappearance. As an official bulletin it was posted up in the town on 20 July, but hastily removed as the Whites advanced. It said unequivocally: 'The family of Romanov has been taken to another and safer place.'

But rumours soon arose that the entire family had been put up against the wall in the Ipatiev House and shot dead. Then, so went the stories, their bodies had been destroyed by being soaked with acid and burned on bonfires at an abandoned mine outside the town.

In fact, this version was put out by the White forces that took the town about a week after the Bolsheviks' bulletin. As evidence for the massacre, they produced photographs of the basement complete with bullet marks. The floors were discoloured as though bloodstains had been washed off hastily.

At the abandoned Ganin mine in the Four Brothers woods some distance to the north of

Right: Ipatiev House, the home of an Ekaterinburg professor used as a prison for the Romanovs. Two high fences were built around the house after the Romanovs were brought here

Right: the Imperial family as prisoners in Siberia. After their transfer to Tobolsk from house arrest at one of their palaces, their imprisonment took on a harsher form

Below right: this bullet-torn wall in the Ipatiev House was said to be the scene of the Romanovs' death in the accepted version of the shooting of the Imperial family

the town, jewels and other artefacts identified as having belonged to the Romanovs were found with piles of ashes, some false teeth and a human thumb. There were also several metal stays from corsets of the kind worn by the Tsarina and her daughters. Apart from the thumb – later tentatively identified as that of the family doctor – no other human remains of any kind were discovered.

On the whole, modern informed opinion tends to side, if only broadly, with the Bolshevik version. The 'corroborative' evidence of the killings found at Four Brothers – corsets, identifiable jewels, and so on – seems rather too obvious, particularly in view of the absence of any human remains apart from the thumb and a scrap or two of skin.

It is notoriously difficult to destroy a human body completely, particularly on an open fire, for the heat simply chars the outer

surface while leaving the remnants even less combustible. Similarly, a body would have to be immersed in strong acid for some weeks to destroy it, and even then bone fragments and teeth would remain. (Teeth are virtually indestructible, whether by fire, acid, or natural decay after death.) As an aid to burning the bodies, pouring acid over them would not only be ineffectual but also positively dangerous to those trying to burn the remains, for powerfully poisonous fumes would be given off.

The White Russian faction may have known this, but it was in their own interests to foster the story of the cold-blooded massacre. The majority of Russian peasants, despite the Revolution, had a deep quasi-religious awe of the Tsar, and the knowledge of his brutal murder might even then have turned them against Lenin's new order. For

his part, Lenin had good reason to keep at least some of the family alive as possible trump cards in the international diplomatic game. The Romanovs were closely related to most of the European ruling houses including both the Kaiser Wilhelm of Germany, with whom White Russia was at war, and King George V of Britain, with whom it was allied.

During the course of research for a BBC film in the early 1970s, television journalists Anthony Summers and Tom Mangold uncovered a mass of information that they later used for an exhaustive book. Both film and book were called *The file on the Tsar*. The file had been gathered – and later, rather unaccountably, suppressed – by the White Russian faction. It contained strong corroborative evidence that the Tsarina and her daughters had been spirited away from Ekaterinburg in a special train with its windows blacked out. According to reliable British information, this train had been waiting in a siding at Ekaterinburg for some time. On the night of the alleged massacre, and with the White forces actually shelling the town, the train had steamed off in the direction of Perm, about 100 miles (160 kilometres) away to the west.

For eight months after that, reports were filed by, among others, a doctor, railway officials and local Soviet officials to the effect that the Romanov women were living at Perm in squalid conditions and under close guard. Anastasia, it seems, had made several unsuccessful attempts to escape. The Perm doctor, Pavel Ivanovich Utkin, had sworn a deposition in February 1919 that in the previous September he had been called to a tenement room by Red Army soldiers and asked to attend a young woman. Apparently the victim of an assault, she had cuts and bruises about the face and head, and was trembling violently though unconscious. As Dr Utkin examined her, she woke up.

A startling revelation

'I asked her: "Who are you?"' Dr Utkin said. 'In a trembling voice, but quite distinctly, she answered me, word for word – as follows: "I am the Emperor's daughter, Anastasia." '

Fyodor Sitnikova, a soldier from Perm serving with the 5th Tomsk-Siberian Regiment, had been on leave that September. He gave testimony on how Anastasia was caught as she tried to run away:

I learned from some Red Army men who were there that they had just caught a daughter of the former Tsar, Anastasia, at the fringe of the woods . . . . I asked how it had happened, and the Red Army men told me they had gone into the woods to do a little shooting, caught sight of a woman walking at the edge of the woods, shouted to her to stop, but she ran off. They fired and she fell. Then they arrested her and brought her here . . . .

These and other statements were collected during the first part of 1919 by Alexander Kirsta, assistant head of White Military Control at Perm, acting under the instructions of General Rudolf Gaida, Czech commander-in-chief of the White Army in the Urals.

The documents were last in the possession of Nikolai Sokolov, who was also the last person in charge of the investigation. He failed to publish them. Instead he produced a book containing the biased version that has become accepted as history. But the monarchist Sokolov guarded the unpublished documents jealously, and took them out of Russia when the Whites were finally routed by the Reds in the late summer of 1919. Summers and Mangold found them in the University of Harvard library, and in California uncovered several other documents relevant to the travels of the Romanov family. But even with these, the Romanov trail petered out at Perm in mid 1919. The final fate of the Romanovs remains a mystery – with perhaps one exception.

This brings us back to the nameless young woman who was the subject of the Berlin police bulletin on 18 February 1920. Taken to hospital after her attempted suicide, she stubbornly refused to identify herself during her six-week stay. Then she was transferred to the Dalldorf Insane Asylum for observation, spending the next two years there. During that time, she was almost totally withdrawn from everything going on around her, and she consistently refused to answer any questions put by the authorities. Nonetheless, she was not declared insane.

And this despite the fact that she had confided in some of the nurses that she was the missing Grand Duchess Anastasia Nikolayevna Romanova.

Above: as a patient in a mental hospital, this woman stubbornly resisted all attempts to learn who she was – then she began to tell the nurses that she was none other than the Grand Duchess Anastasia

Above right: 'Anastasia' in 1968, six days after her marriage to John Manahan, who gave her security and protection in her last years. While living in Charlottesville, Virginia, as an American citizen, she was out of the public eye after nearly 50 years of constant publicity

Anastasia: riches to rags

Did the sole surviving member of the Imperial family of Russia live quietly in an American university town? This is one possibility suggested by the tangled evidence of the Anastasia case

THE NURSES at the Dalldorf Insane Asylum, one of Berlin's principal mental hospitals, were deeply sympathetic to the unidentified young woman who had been brought there six weeks after attempting suicide in the city's Landwehr Canal in February 1920. And indeed they had every reason to be.

The immersion in the icy water had not helped her already weak lungs, which haemorrhaged slightly and tended towards pleurisy, and she was chronically anaemic. Furthermore, she showed signs of having

Lilli Palmer in the film *Is Anna Anderson Anastasia?* (below), made in Germany, and Ingrid Bergman in *Anastasia* (bottom), made in Hollywood. Both came out in the 1950s, when interest in Anna Anderson's claim to be the Grand Duchess Anastasia was at its peak. She was presumed killed with her family in 1918

suffered severe violence at some time in her unknown past: above her right ear was a groove in the skull, resembling the scar likely to be made by a bullet 'creasing' the bone, and her jaws had been damaged – some of the teeth knocked out, some loosened – as if by beating. The arch and instep of one foot bore triangular scars, as if they had been pierced by a sharp instrument.

The authorities who questioned the blue-eyed, dark-haired girl during her two-year stay at Dalldorf were convinced that she was a Russian refugee, and that fear of repatriation kept her silent. For she either could not or would not answer questions about her past, which was why she had been transferred from the hospital to the asylum. Instead she lay in her bed, eating little and paying scant attention to those around her.

Some of her nurses could, if they had chosen, shed a glimmer of light on the mystery woman, for though she spoke fluent German, she was heard muttering in Russian in her sleep from time to time. Furthermore, she had confided to some of them that she was the Grand Duchess Anastasia who, according to official reports, had been executed with her father the Tsar and the rest of her immediate family in the summer of 1918.

But it was one of her fellow patients who first brought her to the notice of the outside world as a possible member of the Imperial Romanovs. In March 1922 Clara Peuthert,

who had lived in Moscow before the revolution, was discharged from Dalldorf. Soon after, she told a former White Russian officer that she thought she had recognised the Grand Duchess Tatiana, Anastasia's older sister, among the inmates of the mental hospital. Apparently she had not spoken to the patient calling herself Anastasia.

As a result of this conversation, a former police officer from Russian Poland, Baron Arthur von Kleist, visited the mystery woman and spent two months gaining her confidence. He then secured her release and took her into his own home. According to him, she told him – in a confidence that he quickly broke – that she was Anastasia. She recounted that she had made her escape from Russia under the protection of a soldier by the name of Alexander Tschaikowsky, who had later been killed. In a mood of black despair, she had made her own way to Berlin where she had tried to kill herself.

By July 1922 Baron von Kleist had broken the news – and 'Anastasia' entered a glare of publicity that was to surround her for the next half century. It is worthy of note that, while privately asserting her Romanov identity, the woman last known as Anna Manahan has never personally attempted to

Anna Anderson as she began her sheltered years as the wife of the American professor Dr John Manahan (standing). Gleb Botkin, son of Tsar Nicholas II's doctor and staunch supporter of Anna's right to the name of Anastasia, was a witness at the wedding in 1967. By then, Anna had been through nearly 50 years of publicity and controversy – with no resolution to the court case deliberating whether she was really the last of the Imperial Romanovs of Russia

persuade the outside world of it. Her 'case' has always been in the hands of others. In fact, her reaction to von Kleist's revelation was to run away from his care, and for the next five years she was in and out of hospitals – and the world's press.

One of the dozens of people who visited Anastasia – among them members of the Romanov clan – was Tatiana Botkin, daughter of the Tsar's doctor who had presumably perished with the Imperial family. Tatiana Botkin arrived determined to expose the 'impostor'. Instead, despite the nameless woman's gaunt appearance, she immediately recognised her as Anastasia.

The German authorities seemed also to be convinced. In 1926 'Anastasia' was advised to go to Switzerland for medical reasons, and the German Foreign Ministry instructed the Berlin Aliens Office to issue her with an identity card, although bureaucratically she did not exist, alluding to 'special reasons' for doing so. A senior official at the Prussian Home Office said that '. . . on the basis of police enquiries so far, the unknown woman is in all probability one and the same as the Tsar's daughter Anastasia.'

Sinister opposition

In 1925 the Tsar's mother, Dowager Empress Marie, who was living in exile at the Danish court, asked her brother Prince Valdemar of Denmark to look into the affair. He instructed Herluf Zahle, then Danish ambassador in Berlin as well as the president of the League of Nations, to conduct enquiries. After a time Zahle also became convinced that 'Anastasia' was genuine, but he found the German relatives – the Tsarina's side of the family – obstructive. Grand Duke Andrei, a senior Romanov, a trained jurist and the Tsar's cousin, also undertook an investigation. He met with the same opposition, so much so that he began to think there was something sinister behind it. Grand Duke Ernst Ludwig of Hesse, the Tsarina's brother, had told Andrei that his enquiries could be 'perilous', which prompted Andrei to write in one of his letters: '. . . it is plain to see that "they" fear something and are very disturbed, as if the investigation could uncover something embarrassing and even dangerous for them. . . .'

Certainly the Grand Duke of Hesse made a number of fumbling attempts to discredit the claimant. At the same time, one of the other cousins, Duke George of Leuchtenberg, invited her to stay at his castle in Upper Bavaria, which she did. Then in 1928 she went to New York as the guest of Princess Xenia Georgievna, the real Anastasia's second cousin. There she changed her name to Anna Anderson to escape the press ballyhoo. There she also became involved in an ill-advised court action under the irresponsible guidance of Gleb Botkin, son of the Tsar's doctor.

The repercussions sent Anna to Germany

again in 1931 and to another mental hospital. Befriended by a Romanov cousin while there, she spent the next 13 years in relative peace as the guest of many of Europe's aristocracy.

Meanwhile, a legal wrangle began in earnest in 1933. It started over who exactly was to get the Tsar's legendary fortune, allegedly distributed among banks in various countries. The only money ever actually discovered was in Germany – and was far from a fortune. But in 1937 the courts ruled that it could be divided among a named number of the Tsar's near relatives. One of the legal documents mentioned that Anastasia was 'deceased', and, scrupulously fair, the bank holding the money wrote to Anna Anderson to warn her. Her lawyers, recommended and provided by friends, found her a reluctant client. But they entered the long – and

Above: Serge Lifar (right), world-famous ballet dancer, choreographer and writer, testified in the Anastasia court case in 1958

Left: Marie, Dowager Empress of Russia and grandmother of the real Anastasia. She instituted an investigation of Anna Anderson but never saw the claimant in person

Below: the Grand Duke of Hesse, one of the German relations of the Romanovs. He refused to consider the possibility that Anna Anderson was his cousin

'presumed' the death of Anastasia. The late Lord Mountbatten, his sister Princess Andrew of Greece – mother of Prince Philip – and Queen Louise of Sweden were among the likely defendants, but instead the choice fell on two German cousins from the line of Hesse. From 1957 until 1970 the case was almost continuously before the German courts and, as the journalists Anthony Summers and Tom Mangold remarked in their book *The file on the Tsar*: 'Given that there is supposedly no Romanov fortune at stake, the Tsar's relatives in exile went to extraordinary lengths to smother the Anastasia affair.'

One reason for this could well be a collective sense of guilt by royal relatives who made little if any attempt to rescue the Imperial family through diplomatic means. For example, documents exist showing that King George V quashed a tentative British plan to save his cousin Nicholas – perhaps out of concern that his position would be in

ultimately inconclusive – fight as a way to establish her legal identity more than for the inheritance.

During the Second World War Anna Anderson was trapped in Soviet Russia, undoubtedly a nightmare experience if she was who she claimed to be. After the war she became increasingly eccentric, settling as a hermit in the Black Forest in a hut bought for her, and living with an elderly female companion, a host of cats, and four ferocious wolfhounds.

But the spotlight was still on her. A German feature film, starring Lilli Palmer and dealing with 'Anastasia's' fight for recognition, was followed by the glittering Hollywood version starring Ingrid Bergman. The world's press literally beat a path through the woods to her humble door, while the fresh publicity brought a new legal turn. The Berlin Court of Appeal, on turning down her lawyers' appeal for her legal recognition, suggested that she sue those who had

jeopardy if he championed the Tsar.

But another reason for the opposition to 'Anastasia's' claims, particularly from the Germans, may well tell in her favour. While gravely ill in hospital in 1926, Anna implored a visitor, the widow of a German dignitary, to bring the Grand Duke of Hesse – her 'Uncle Ernie' as she called him – to her bedside. She said she had last seen him 'in the war, with us, at home'. To the visitor and others present this seemed impossible, for Russia and Germany had been at war and Grand Duke Ernst Ludwig had been an active German general. When this woman did visit the Grand Duke and did mention this conversation, he immediately turned cold and told her that he could not become involved. Later, despite scepticism amounting almost to scorn, 'Anastasia' made the claim again, to Herluf Zahle. 'Uncle Ernie' she said, had paid a secret visit to the Tsar in 1916 to attempt to arrange a separate peace between Russia and Germany.

Vindication for Anna Anderson came from a highly respectable source in 1953 when Crown Princess Cecile, the Kaiser's daughter-in-law, swore a formal deposition:

If the view is still held today that such a visit never took place, I can assert from personal knowledge – the source is my late father-in-law – that this visit was already known in our circles at the time. In my opinion [Anna] showed by her statement, which I only heard about much later, strong evidence at least of her intimate knowledge of the high politics and of the most secret dealings of the Imperial family.

Since then other depositions and documents have come to light making the secret trip

Top: the house in the Bavarian Black Forest where Anna Anderson sought to escape the glare of publicity

Above: Crown Princess Cecile of Germany, whose father-in-law was Kaiser Wilhelm II, another Romanov cousin. She gave testimony favourable to Anna Anderson in 1953

almost a certainty. In view of this, the opposition of the Grand Duke and many of his close German family, who always hoped for a restoration of the German monarchy, is understandable. Proof of such an act would have been a sword in the hands of German republicans, though as Summers and Mangold have said, it seems odd that they still opposed Anna Anderson even after their hopes must have died.

In 1918 the real Anastasia was described as 'plump and pretty'. By 1922 the claimant to her name had undergone great hardship and was almost skeletal. Yet despite her physical change, many members of her 'family' recognised her as their supposedly dead 'kin'. Grand Duke Andrei, for instance, was quite convinced. The Tsar's sister Olga, who saw the real Anastasia only rarely, was partially convinced but could never make up her mind, while Prince Sigismund of Prussia, her companion in childhood, knew who she was without having seen her. When 'Anastasia' first surfaced, Sigismund was in central America, so he sent the claimant a list of personal questions that only the real Anastasia could answer correctly. Anna answered all of them accurately.

The court files amount to almost 8000 foolscap pages – but no decision as to Anastasia's identity has been made. Anna had ceased to be personally involved, and after a short period in a mental hospital she died in early 1984. She had stopped caring long ago and in 1977 – weary of the neverending publicity – she wrote a personal letter to a press agency formally declaring that she was closing the case for good. And the question of whether she was the real Anastasia remains a puzzle of history.

The classic case of 'Mary Celeste'

The abrupt disappearance of *Mary Celeste*'s entire crew is one of the most fascinating mysteries of the sea. But, as PAUL BEGG points out, that was only the climax of a long history of weird misfortunes

ON 5 DECEMBER 1872 a crewman on watch on board the British ship *Dei Gratia* sighted a vessel that seemed to be in distress. Three seamen lowered the *Dei Gratia*'s small boat and rowed across to the troubled craft to offer assistance. They hauled themselves over the ship's rails and dropped onto the deck; save for the sound of the wind in the sails and the eerie creaking of the ship's timbers, there was not a sound. The seamen searched the ship from stem to stern and found her to be in excellent condition, but there was not a soul on board. Her crew had disappeared. The name of the ship was *Mary Celeste*.

The disappearance of her crew is the central element in *Mary Celeste*'s long history of misfortune. She attracted bad luck like a magnet attracts iron filings. The superstitious would call her jinxed, and *Mary Celeste*'s story is one that would make even a hard-boiled sceptic agree that the superstitious might have a point.

Mary Celeste was built in 1860, the maiden venture of a consortium of pioneer shipbuilders at the shipyards of Joshua Dewis on Spencer's Island, Nova Scotia. She was originally christened *Amazon* and was launched in 1861, the year that saw the start of the American Civil War. Tragedy struck a short while later when her first skipper, a Scot named Robert McLellan, fell ill and died. Then one John Nutting Parker assumed command and skippered the *Amazon*'s maiden voyage, but she ran into a fishing weir off Maine, received a large gash in her hull and had to go to the shipyards for repair. While she was there a fire broke out amidships, bringing Captain Parker's short-lived command to an end.

Amazon's first Atlantic crossing went without mishap until she entered the Straits of Dover and collided with a brig. The brig sank, *Amazon* again went for repairs, and her third skipper went to seek another command.

Following the necessary repairs and the appointment of a new captain, *Amazon* returned to America, and she promptly ran aground off Cow Bay, Cape Breton Island, Nova Scotia.

Amazon's history now becomes a little hazy. She was pulled off the rocks and repaired, but appears to have passed from

Right: the *Mary Celeste*, the Nova Scotian half-brig whose name is synonymous with the most bizarre kind of disappearance

Above: J. H. Winchester, one of the owners of the hapless sailing ship that eventually became the *Mary Celeste*

Below: the *Amazon*, built in 1860 in Nova Scotia. Until she became the *Mary Celeste* a few years later, her short career was 'unlucky'; but afterwards it was disastrous

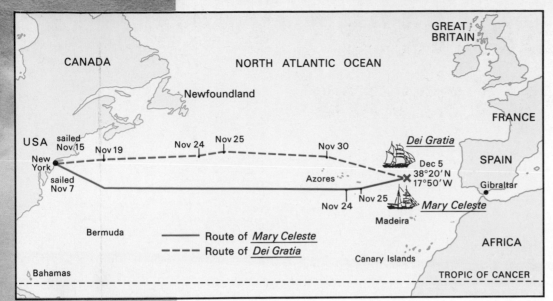

CANADA

NORTH ATLANTIC OCEAN

GREAT BRITAIN

Newfoundland

FRANCE

USA
sailed Nov 15

New York

sailed Nov 7

Nov 19   Nov 24   Nov 25   Nov 30

Azores

Dei Gratia

Dec 5
38°20′N
17°50′W

SPAIN

Gibraltar

Nov 24   Nov 25

Madeira

Mary Celeste

Bermuda   —— Route of *Mary Celeste*
- - - Route of *Dei Gratia*

AFRICA

Canary Islands

TROPIC OF CANCER

Bahamas

Left: map showing the respective routes of the *Dei Gratia* and the *Mary Celeste* during November and December 1872. X marks the spot where the crew of the *Dei Gratia* sighted the bedraggled sailing ship, apparently becalmed and showing no sign of life

one owner to another, several of whom seem to have gone bankrupt and none of whom derived any good from their contact with the ship. She eventually passed into the hands of J.H. Winchester and Co., a consortium of New York shipowners. By this time the *Amazon* was unrecognisable as the vessel that had left the shipyards of Joshua Dewis. She had been enlarged, now flew the Stars and Stripes, and on her nameboard was *Mary Celeste*. It has been suggested that the peculiar mixture of English and French names was the result of the painter's error, the intended name being *Mary Sellers* or even perhaps *Marie Celeste*, the name, ironically, by which most people know her.

Sometime during late September or early October in 1872 *Mary Celeste* was berthed at Pier 44 in New York's East River, preparing to take on a new cargo and a fresh crew.

Benjamin Spooner Briggs

The latest captain of *Mary Celeste* was a stern, puritan New Englander named Benjamin Spooner Briggs. He was born at Wareham, Massachusetts, on 24 April 1835, the second of five sons born to Captain Nathan Briggs and his wife Sophia. It was a seafaring family; apart from his father, four of his brothers also went to sea. Two became master mariners at an early age, one of them being Benjamin Briggs, who had already commanded the schooner *Forest King*, the barque *Arthur*, and the brigantine *Sea Foam*. In later years many authors painted him as weak and ineffectual, a man whose religious beliefs had become a form of perversion, a mania, turning his strict abstinence from alcohol – which went so far as to allow none on board his ship unless it were cargo – into something akin to over-zealous morality. Briggs was in fact a man of strict beliefs and religious convictions, and although he was a teetotaller he was no monomaniac on the subject. He was described by those who knew him as always bearing 'the highest

character as a Christian and as an intelligent and active shipmaster'. He was also a shareholder in the *Mary Celeste*.

The first mate was Albert G. Richardson. A soldier in the American Civil War, he had married a niece of James H. Winchester's and had served before with Captain Briggs. He seems to have been trustworthy and competent and was held in high esteem.

Andrew Gilling was the second mate. His birthplace was given as New York but he seems to have been of Danish extraction. Again there is no reason to suspect that he was other than upright and honest.

The cook and steward, Edward William Head, hailed from Brooklyn, New York, where it is said that he was respected by all.

The remainder of the crew consisted of four seamen of German birth, about whom little is known except that two of them – both named Lorenzen – had lost all their possessions when shipwrecked prior to signing on as crewmen on *Mary Celeste*. None of these Germans appears to have been anything other than of good character.

Also making the voyage into the unknown were Captain Briggs's wife, Sarah Elizabeth – the daughter of the preacher of the Congregational Church in Marion, Massachusetts – and one of their two children, two-year-old Sophia Matilda. The elder child, their son Arthur Stanley, remained at home.

Late on Saturday, 2 November 1872 *Mary Celeste*'s cargo was loaded and made secure. She carried 1701 barrels of denatured alcohol being shipped by Meissner Ackerman and Co., merchants of New York, to H. Mascerenhas and Co., of Genoa, Italy.

Early on 5 November the Sandy Hook pilot ship towed *Mary Celeste* from Pier 44 to the lower bay off Staten Island, New York. The Atlantic was particularly stormy for the time of year and Briggs was forced to drop anchor for two days before he dared to venture out to sea on 7 November. But although *Mary Celeste* herself would make many more voyages, it was the last time anyone would see this particular crew.

On 15 November 1872, eight days after *Mary Celeste* left New York, *Dei Gratia* set off with a cargo of petroleum bound for Gibraltar. Her skipper was a Nova Scotian named David Reed Morehouse and the first mate was Oliver Deveau. Both these men and the rest of *Dei Gratia*'s crew were highly able sailors – as later events were to prove – and no 'dirt' has ever been attached to their characters except by sensationalists.

On 5 December, shortly after 1 p.m., one of the *Dei Gratia*'s crew, John Johnson, who was at the wheel, sighted a vessel about 5 miles (8 kilometres) off the port bow. Attracted by the poor state of the ship's sails and her slight 'yawing' (listing), he called the second mate, John Wright, and together they summoned Captain Morehouse. After surveying the vessel through his telescope, Morehouse gave orders to offer assistance.

At 3 p.m., having come within about 400 yards (370 metres) of the mystery ship, Morehouse hailed her several times, but, receiving no reply from her, he decided to send some men to investigate.

Oliver Deveau, with Wright and Johnson, rowed across to the distressed craft, noting as they drew closer, its name – *Mary Celeste*. Johnson was left in the boat as the other two hauled themselves over the ship's rails. The *Mary Celeste* was deserted.

Over the next hour Deveau and Wright searched *Mary Celeste* from stem to stern. The main staysail was found on the foreward house, but the foresail and upper foresail had been blown from the yards and lost. The jib, fore-topmast staysail and the fore lower topsail were set. The remaining sails were furled. Some of the running rigging was

Top left: Captain Benjamin Spooner Briggs, master of the *Mary Celeste*. A puritan and abstemious New Englander, his alleged religious fanaticism has been blamed for whatever disaster hit the crew – mutiny or madness perhaps

Top right: Briggs's wife, Sarah Elizabeth who, with their two-year-old daughter Sophia Matilda, also sailed on the fatal voyage

Above: the first mate, Albert G. Richardson, who had served before under Briggs and was deemed an excellent seaman

Left: the ship's list, giving the names of those who sailed – and were doomed to vanish without trace

Reproduced from the original in the National Archives (Records of the Department of the Treasury, Bureau of Customs), Washington, D.C.

fouled, some had been blown away, and parts of it were hanging over the sides. The main peak halyard – a stiff rope about 100 yards (90 metres) long used to hoist the outer end of the gaff sail – was broken and most of it missing. The wheel was spinning free and the binnacle had been knocked over and broken. The main hatch to below decks was well-battened down and secure, but certain of the hatch covers had apparently been removed and were found discarded near the hatchways. There was less than a foot (30 centimetres) of water in the galley and little of the six months' store of provisions had been spoilt. There was ample fresh water.

In short, *Mary Celeste* was in a far better condition than most vessels then regularly plying the Atlantic. And, aside from some evidence that she had recently weathered a storm, she bore no clues as to why she had been so abruptly abandoned by her crew.

On a table in Captain Briggs's cabin Oliver Deveau found the temporary log. It read: 'Monday, 25th. At five o'clock made island of St Mary's bearing ESE. At eight o'clock Eastern point bore SSW six miles [3 kilometres] distant.'

In the mate's cabin Deveau found a chart showing the track of the vessel up to 24 November.

Missing from the ship were the chronometer, sextant, bill of lading, navigation book, and a small yawl, or boat, that had been lashed to the main hatch. A piece of railing running alongside had been removed to launch the boat. This at least answered the mystery of where *Mary Celeste*'s crew had gone; they had abandoned ship. But why? What possible reason could an experienced seaman like Benjamin Spooner Briggs have had for abandoning a perfectly seaworthy ship and loading his wife and two-year-old daughter and the seven members of crew into a small and comparatively unstable boat? Abandoning ship is a desperate measure, an act taken only when there is no alternative; yet as one of *Dei Gratia*'s crew said later, *Mary Celeste* was in a fit enough state to sail around the world. So why was she abandoned?

Under international maritime law anyone who salvages an abandoned vessel is entitled to a percentage of what the vessel and its cargo are worth. Generally such a vessel is a wreck, but *Mary Celeste*, a seaworthy ship, and her valuable cargo were worth a substantial sum, and the salvors could expect to make perhaps as much as $80,000. Captain Morehouse was not consumed by avarice, as many subsequent writers have implied, and was actually reluctant to lay claim to *Mary Celeste*. He could not really spare the men to form a skeleton crew without both vessels being undermanned and therefore at risk in the event of an emergency; but he was eventually persuaded by Deveau.

Deveau and two seamen, Augustus Anderson and Charles Lund, took only two days to restore *Mary Celeste* to order, and then the two ships set off for Gibraltar. *Dei Gratia* arrived on the evening of 12 December and *Mary Celeste* the following morning. Within two hours of dropping anchor *Mary Celeste* was placed under arrest by Thomas J. Vecchio, of the Vice-Admiralty Court.

The Attorney General for Gibraltar and Advocate General for the Queen in Her Office of Admiralty was an excitable, arrogant and pompous bureaucrat named Frederick Solly Flood; he found the abandonment of *Mary Celeste* explicable only as a result of murder and piracy. Without Solly Flood the

Oliver Deveau, first mate of the *Dei Gratia*, who, with only two other crewmen, brought the *Mary Celeste* into Gibraltar in December 1872. The British authorities refused to believe their story of how they had discovered *Mary Celeste*

Below: Captain David Reed Morehouse, master of the *Dei Gratia* (bottom). Under maritime law anyone who salvages an abandoned ship is entitled to a handsome percentage of its total worth. In the case of *Mary Celeste* this would have been considerable for she was in excellent condition and had her full complement of cargo. However, Morehouse was reluctant to lay any such claim and found it hard to spare crew to look after *Mary Celeste*. Yet some critics still maintain that Briggs and Morehouse were conspirators, who, having set up the 'disappearances', planned to split the salvage money between them – and live in luxury

Mary Celeste mystery would have probably faded into obscurity, but his accusations at the hearings in the Vice-Admiralty Court attracted worldwide publicity.

First, Flood accused *Mary Celeste*'s original crew – in their absence – of having gained access to the cargo of alcohol and having murdered Captain Briggs, his wife and child, and Mate Richardson in a drunken fury. It is a theory that has been proposed several times since, once by William A. Richard, Secretary of the Treasury of the United States, in an open letter published on the front page of the *New York Times* in 1873. The fact remains that the cargo was denatured alcohol and liable to give the drinker acute pains long before he could become intoxicated. Flood was forced to abandon his theory.

He next suggested that Briggs and Morehouse were conspirators. Briggs, said Flood, killed his crew and disposed of their bodies. He then took the lifeboat to a destination prearranged with Captain Morehouse, who in the meantime would have found *Mary Celeste* abandoned, taken her to Gibraltar and claimed the salvage reward. The two men would then meet and split their ill-gotten gains. This theory is just plausible, but there was and is no evidence that Briggs or Morehouse were villains. Moreover, Briggs was part-owner of *Mary Celeste* and his cut of the salvage money would not have been more than his investment in the vessel. Flood abandoned this idea too.

Guilty until proved innocent

His third suggestion was that Captain Morehouse and the crew of *Dei Gratia* had boarded *Mary Celeste* and savagely slaughtered all on board. Flood tried very hard to make his claim stick, but all he succeeded in doing was generating an atmosphere of suspicion in which Morehouse and his crew would be considered guilty until they could prove themselves innocent. Fortunately, the Vice-Admiralty Court denounced such a flagrant abuse of the law and cleared Morehouse and his crew of any suspicion. They granted them a salvage reward of £1700. In the opinion of many people the award should have been twice or three times as much.

Mary Celeste was returned to James H. Winchester and, under the command of Captain George W. Blatchford, she continued her voyage to Genoa and finally delivered her cargo. Winchester then sold the ship – it is rumoured at a considerable loss – and over the next 12 years the vessel changed hands no less than 17 times. None of her new owners had a good word to say about her. She lurched up and down the coast of the United States losing cargoes, sails and sailors, running aground and catching fire with depressing regularity. It seemed that *Mary Celeste*'s jinx was there to stay.

Voyage into the unknown

Still-warm tea on the galley table, lifeboats all secure – and the crew of the *Mary Celeste* had vanished. Thanks to a deluge of fictional stories, this has become the legend. But what really happened?

IT DID NOT TAKE LONG for the myth surrounding the disappearance of the *Mary Celeste*'s crew to be born. Indeed, it could be argued that it began in Gibraltar in 1872 when Solly Flood tried in vain to attach guilt to Captain Morehouse and the crew of the *Dei Gratia*. But the story was seized upon by writers and journalists and soon caught the public imagination.

The first major piece of fiction about the ship was published in January 1884 by the prestigious *Cornhill Magazine*, 11 months before Gilman C. Parker deliberately burnt the ship (see box on page 83). It was a sensational short story called *J. Habakuk Jephson's statement* and it bore little resemblance to the actual facts. It was picked up by American newspapers however and published as fact, much to the outrage of Solly Flood and Horatio Sprague, the US Consul in Gibraltar, both of whom wrote letters condemning the tale.

Apart from its literary worth, *J. Habakuk Jephson's statement* is interesting for two reasons: it was one of the first literary efforts of a young English doctor named Arthur Conan Doyle, and in it *Mary Celeste* is called *Marie Celeste*, the name by which the ship is

Above: crewmen of the *Dei Gratia* sight the mystery ship *Mary Celeste*, in a painting by Gordon A. Johnson. This was commissioned in 1965 by the Atlantic Mutual Insurance Company – the original insurers of the *Mary Celeste*

now most commonly known. However, Conan Doyle was not the first to make the error – this version of the name first appears in *Lloyd's List* of 25 March 1873.

Conan Doyle's story was the first of many fictional accounts that have appeared over the years; for example, a novel based on the mystery was published as recently as 1980. Some of these tales have been presented as straight fiction, others as fictionalised fact (but nevertheless proposing a serious explanation), and quite a few have been intended to be taken as fact.

In the late 1920s *Chamber's Journal* published an article by Lee Kaye purporting to be a true account of what happened aboard *Mary Celeste* as supposedly told by a survivor named John Pemberton (one of the many 'survivors' who have popped up over the years but whose names are mysteriously absent from the crew list).

Pemberton's story was expanded to book length by Laurence J. Keating in 1929 and called *The great Mary Celeste hoax*. It was a bestseller on both sides of the Atlantic; John Pemberton rapidly became the man of the moment. Many journalists sought interviews with him, but Pemberton remained elusive until a 'special correspondent' of the London *Evening Standard* tracked him down – and obtained not only the coveted interview but a photograph as well. Both were published in the *Evening Standard* on 6 May 1929.

However, one of the few true statements

vessel's crew among the victims of whatever unexplained force they consider to exist in the area, imbuing that force with a singular selectivity, and in the process enlarging the Triangle so that it reaches the Azores. A superficially acceptable theory put forward by a number of rational people was that the food or drinking water was contaminated and caused the crew to hallucinate, driving them mad so that they threw themselves over the side. But Oliver Deveau and other members of the *Dei Gratia*'s crew used the food and water they found aboard *Mary Celeste* and suffered no ill effects.

The United States Consul in Gibraltar, Horatio Sprague, wrote in July 1887 that:

> This case of the *Mary Celeste* is startling, since it appears to be one of those mysteries which no human ingenuity can penetrate sufficiently to account for the abandonment of this vessel and the disappearance of her master, family and crew. . . .

No solution so far offered seems to account for all the circumstances, but it is possible to list some salient facts that might provide a few clues: *Mary Celeste* was abandoned by her captain and crew; those who abandoned ship did so in the ship's yawl. This small vessel would have been overloaded and easily capsized, so the crew's fate is not wholly inexplicable. The ship was abandoned in a hurry: extra clothing was not taken nor – as far as is known – was any food or water, but the crew did not abandon ship in a complete panic, since they took the time to collect the sextant, chronometer, and the ship's papers (apart from the temporary log). Since there was no evidence that *Mary Celeste* had suffered any damage, whatever made the crew abandon her was something they feared had happened or was about to happen, but clearly never did.

The part-owner of the ship, James H. Winchester, suggested that *Mary Celeste*'s cargo of denatured alcohol gave off fumes, which collected in the hold and formed an explosive mixture. This, he speculated, was

in Keating's book was its title: the story *was* a hoax; Lee Kaye, Laurence Keating, and the *Evening Standard*'s 'special correspondent' were all one and the same person, an Irish-Liverpudlian named Laurence J. Keating. John Pemberton was a figment of Keating's fertile imagination and the photograph of 'Pemberton' was of Keating's own father.

While the majority of theories to explain the abandonment of *Mary Celeste* are generally a variation on the theme of murder – committed either by *Mary Celeste*'s own crew or by the men of *Dei Gratia* – other solutions are not uncommon and are frequently bizarre. The 1900s favoured 'monster from the depths' stories in which *Mary Celeste* was attacked by a huge hungry octopus that plucked the entire crew from the deck. Although it has its attractions for illustrators, the theory also has a number of flaws. Even if such a huge and vicious creature exists it is highly unlikely that everyone aboard *Mary Celeste* would have been on deck at the same time or that they would have obligingly stayed there as the monster plucked them off one by one. We must also assume that for some reason it craved *Mary Celeste*'s yawl, chronometer, sextant, and ship's papers.

The late Morris K. Jessup, who was involved with the alleged Philadelphia experiment (see page 60), suggested that *Mary Celeste*'s crew were abducted by a UFO. And Bermuda Triangle writers list the

Above: the alleged suicide of the *Marie Celeste*'s captain – 'Tibbs' – from an illustration of Conan Doyle's story *J. Habakuk Jephson's statement*. A gripping tale, it was taken by many to be true and popularised the misnomer '*Marie*' Celeste

Below: sea monsters have also been blamed for the tragedy

Dr James H. Kimble, once the head of the United States Weather Bureau in New York, and author Gershom Bradford have both suggested that *Mary Celeste* was struck by a waterspout, a tornado at sea; a column of whirling wind and water that can appear without warning, last for up to an hour, and then break up as quickly as it appeared.

At first glance this theory does not seem very plausible, particularly as waterspouts are not common outside the tropics, nor is it common for ships to be struck by them. But the fact is that waterspouts are not totally restricted to the tropics: for example, in December 1920 the steamer *British Marquis* reported no less than 20 waterspouts in the English Channel.

Mr Bradford and Dr Kimble believe that a relatively small and harmless spout, narrow and travelling at an angle, could have struck the ship without doing a great deal of damage; indeed, it would have left the vessel no worse than had she encountered a storm. All this is consistent with the state of *Mary Celeste* when first sighted by the *Dei Gratia*. However, within a waterspout the barometric pressure is extremely low and, as the spout passed over the ship, the marked difference in pressure between the inside and outside of the ship could have caused the hatch covers to blow off – in the same way that a building's walls explode outward when struck by a tornado.

In this context, the method by which *Mary Celeste* was sounded may be extremely significant. This was done by dropping a rod down the pump well to measure the water in the hold, in much the same way as a motorist checks his oil with a dipstick. The drop in barometric pressure could have driven the bilge water up the pump-well, where a valve

either ignited by a spark, resulting, perhaps, from friction caused by the metal bands around the barrels rubbing together, or a naked light used during cargo inspection. Or perhaps the fumes had been mistaken for smoke and gave rise to the belief that the ship was about to be blown out of the water.

Experts have expressed the opinion that there could have been no *visible* vapour, but that an explosive mixture could have been formed. However, this would not have resulted in a minor explosion, but would have blown *Mary Celeste* into matchwood.

The most likely solution was in part offered by Oliver Deveau at the salvage hearing. He said that he thought the crew had panicked, believing that the ship was sinking. It was not an opinion that has impressed many commentators and most have dismissed it as idiotic (and Deveau himself as an idiot). But in fairness to Deveau, his comment has to be taken in context. At the hearing he was asked a straightforward question, and he answered it without elaboration. Later researchers, however, have tried to interpret his meaning.

Above: a reconstruction of one theory about the disappearance of the crew of *Mary Celeste*: they all fell overboard. The influential *Strand Magazine* heard that a reputable schoolmaster had a servant named Abel Fosdyk who claimed to have been the only survivor. Fosdyk said that Captain Briggs went mad. This may or may not be connected with the 'fact' that everyone else on board was precipitated into the sea from a flimsy play area built for the captain's daughter. Fosdyk threw no light on why no one managed to climb back on board

Right: in the 1936 film version the bosun goes mad and kills the entire crew, including himself

C. M. WOOLF
PRESENTS
BELA LUGOSI
SHIRLEY GREY
in
The MYSTERY OF THE MARY CELESTE
with ARTHUR MARGETSON
HAMMER PRODUCTION
Directed by DENISON CLIFT

would have prevented it from returning immediately to the hold. Although this would have been merely a temporary malfunction, the crew may not have realised it.

Suppose, then, that after the waterspout had moved on the crew were shaken and confused. Somebody went to sound the ship to see if she had suffered any underwater damage, and to his horror found that *Mary Celeste* had leaked 6 to 8 feet (2 to 2½ metres) of water in less than a minute – or so the seaman would have thought when he removed the sounding rod. Believing *Mary Celeste* to be sinking fast, Captain Briggs, perhaps panicking out of concern for his wife and daughter, gave the order to abandon ship. Perhaps this was what Oliver Deveau had meant by his cryptic statement. We shall never know, but the waterspout theory certainly seems to fit most of the reported circumstances and also explains the most baffling feature of the case: what monstrous happening threatened those aboard *Mary Celeste*, resulting in their hurried evacuation but still allowing them time in which to grab sextant, chronometer and ship's papers?

One commentator has called the case of *Mary Celeste* 'a detective-story writer's nightmare: the perfectly perplexing situation without any logical solution – a plot which can never be convincingly unravelled.'

On 16 May 1873 the *Daily Albion* of Liverpool reported that two rafts had been found by fishermen at Baudus, in Asturias, near Madrid, Spain. One of the rafts had a corpse lashed to it and was flying an American flag. The second raft bore five decomposing bodies. Curiously, the matter was not investigated, so no one will ever know who they were or what ship they belonged to. But could they have been from *Mary Celeste*?

Above: a waterspout at sea. A fast, angled one could have hit the *Mary Celeste*, causing only superficial damage and temporarily falsifying the crew's soundings. Believing that they were sinking, the crew could have panicked and abandoned ship. Although this is one of the more reasonable theories, it is unlikely that anyone will ever discover the truth

A terrible risk

In late 1884 an ageing and rather unkempt *Mary Celeste* was bought by Gilman C. Parker and loaded with freight, which he insured for $30,000. The vessel then sailed for Port-au-Prince, Haiti. But she never arrived. On 3 January 1885 *Mary Celeste* ran aground on the razor-sharp coral reef of Rochaelais Bank in the Gulf of Gonave, off the coast of Haiti.

Parker put in an insurance claim, but for some reason the insurance companies regarded it with deep suspicion and sent enquiry agents to investigate. They found that Parker had loaded the ship with rubbish – not the valuable cargo he had insured – had deliberately run *Mary Celeste* aground, unloaded the part of the cargo that he could sell, and then set *Mary Celeste* alight.

Parker was charged with barratry –

fraud and/or criminal negligence by a ship's officer or crew against the owners or insurers. In those days this was a crime punishable by death. The case was heard in a federal court in Boston, but it was dropped because of a legal technicality. Gilman C. Parker, a grizzled old sea-dog who was – judging by the evidence – undoubtedly guilty of every maritime crime short of piracy, and his associates walked from the court free men. Free, that is, from the penalties of a court of law, but not from the jinx of *Mary Celeste*. In a short time Parker went bankrupt, and he died in poverty and disrepute. One of his fellow conspirators went insane and was placed in a mental institution where he ended his days. Another killed himself. In the end the jinx of *Mary Celeste* had won, having horribly ruined many lives.